ARE YOU NUTS?!

ARE YOU NUTS?!

▼

And other things you may as well get used to
hearing when you start your own business

Donald J. Willis

Writers Club Press
San Jose New York Lincoln Shanghai

Are You Nuts?!
And other things you may as well get used to hearing
when you start your own business

Writers Club Press
an imprint of iUniverse.com, Inc.

For information address:
iUniverse.com, Inc.
5220 S 16th, Ste. 200
Lincoln, NE 68512
www.iuniverse.com

ISBN: 0-595-17818-9

Printed in the United States of America

CONTENTS

———————▼———————

PREFACE

▼

80% of all businesses that are started fail within the first year. This book is dedicated to placing you in the 20% that survive, by making sure you understand what you are doing when you make the decision to start your own business. So, if, after reading this book, you have steeled yourself against the hard times to come, and still wish to start your own business, then get ready for the ride of your life.

I've often heard 'You never get rich working for somebody else'. It's true enough…with the exceptions of any generality. But many have also driven themselves into bankruptcy starting a business. The failures far outnumber the successes. So, as the Boy Scouts would say…'Be Prepared'.

The main reason new businesses fail is because they are not prepared for what they have gotten themselves into when starting a business. Reading 'How To' books is important in your learning process, but many books on starting a business are loaded with 'Blue Sky' attitudes about how rich you will be following their ideas. I guarantee this book is nothing but gray sky and lightning. So, if you are wanting to be pumped full of hot air, then put this book down. This book isn't about cheerleading…this is to get you ready for the fight of your financial life. It is also to help the squeamish that will read it to realize how difficult it is, and convince them to leave their money in the bank rather than watch their business drain their accounts dry. A war was never won by armies prepared for peace, and this will be a war. You need to see the war that is coming, and prepare yourself for the fight to come. I promise you, starting your own business will be the fight of your life. But, if you are successful, it will be a fight well worth the challenges you will have faced.

CHAPTER ONE

───────▼───────

So you've got it in your head to start a small business. WHY...? Let me guess some of the questions your family and friends have asked since you stated a desire to own your own business:

Are you nuts!?!?!?!?!

Do you want to put us in the poorhouse?!?!?!?!?!

Are you crazy?!?!?!?! (often used in conjunction with the nuts question)

How do you propose we pay the bills...our looks?!?!?!?!

Do you need your head examined?!?!?!?!

(also often used with the nuts and crazy questions)

Are you nuts?!?!?!?!?!? (often used repeatedly)

The number of those questions is directly proportional to the number of days it takes your business to generate a profit, so brace yourself and get used to it. They are, however, legitimate questions, and asking yourself why you want to start your own business is the key first step in deciding whether or not to strike out on your own. Taking pen to paper and listing those reasons can be not only helpful, but necessary to planning your new venture.

I've often said that there are four categories of people:

1. Workers-Most owners started in this category at one time. They trade their labor each week for a paycheck. Our entire system of

commerce is based upon barter. We barter our time and skills in exchange for money from the owner of the company for which we work. In this system of bartering, the owner evaluates the job you are going to perform and comes to the conclusion that your time and labor are worth more money than the amount of money he/she will pay to you for your time and labor.

2. Owners-The vast majority of owners were, at one time, workers with an idea. To paraphrase Calvin Coolidge, "There is nothing more common than a talented man without the courage and drive to utilize that talent." The only thing that separates them from the other workers who have had ideas is that they stepped out onto the ledge and actually jumped, rather than having enough sense to go back inside. In every industry, it is easy to find people who can give you a lot of reasons why it makes no sense for a person to strike out on his/her own. But without those people whom, to so many, have no apparent sense, the workers would have no one with which to barter their labor. The Bible never said, "And on the sixth day God created the Ford Motor Company." It was created by one man with an idea, and there has never been anything on this Earth more powerful than 1 person with an idea and the drive to see it through.

3. Silver Spoons-This group of people inherit their wealth and position in society. Often they belong to neither the worker nor the owner category, and spend their time involved in charities and causes. Whether this is out of some unfounded guilt, or simply because they don't know what to do with all that time they have on their hands is hard to say. When they do venture into the world of owners, it often meets with disaster. The phrase "shirt sleeves to shirt sleeves in 3 generations" was born from the often inevitable failure that occurs. A parent will work hard to build a successful company and family fortune, and turn it over to a child who has had everything growing up. This adult, not knowing the hard work that is necessary, will often

drive the company into failure. On occasion, the silver spoon will recognize his/her own shortcomings, and either put qualified people in place to run the company, sell the company, or roll up their sleeves and truly join the owner category. More often than not, however, they are simply looking for their next tee time.

4. Politicians-This category exists simply to siphon as much money as possible from the owners and the workers. While he or she has their hand in your wallet, they are telling you how they are doing such a great job, and how it's the fault of all the other politicians that they have their hand in your wallet. Owners and workers must show results today or they will fail in what they are doing. Politicians, however, will tell you what a congress of 5 to 10 years from now will do, and claim the credit as if they have already done it themselves. Workers are diligent, owners tend to be bold, but most politicians are cowards when it comes to making tough or right decisions. They are often more worried about getting re-elected than doing what is right for the country. If a business owner played with numbers and cut budgets in 'out years' that never come, he would either be fired or put in jail. Unfortunately, most workers believe something good has happened for them when the so-called 'rich' take the larger tax hit. But…keep in mind, a poor person never hired anybody. An employer has a pie of money to work from, and, as the government's slice gets larger, the employees' slice gets smaller. This often results in downsizing, less or no bonuses, reduced or no salary increases, etc. So, next time you feel like cheering when the tax goes up on the next guy, why not ask the question…. "Why don't all politicians just cut spending?"

Unless you inherit your fortune, you must decide to which category you wish to belong…of the remaining three.

If you still want to move into the uncertain world of 'ownerdom', it's time for you to get that pen and paper. Go ahead….I'll wait…(tapping pencil...humming to myself...looking at watch...) Got it? Good. Now let's start trying to figure out exactly why you want to step off of that ledge.

Circle the ones that apply to you, and try to discover some of your own.

1. Tired of working for someone else? Entrepreneurial people often get bored working for others, and enjoy the challenge of making a business successful.

2. Hate your employer or supervisor? You may want to consider a new job. This is not a very good reason to take the risk of starting your own business.

3. Hate what you do for a living? Try a career change. Find something you enjoy and give it the time you need to discover if you truly have the entrepreneurial spirit...or if you are simply in need of a change.

4. Control your own Destiny? This reason is stated often by entrepreneurs who have, at some time, worked at companies with inept management. There is a strong desire in these people to capture the rewards from their work done well without management's incompetence sending your work into the toilet.

5. Ego? There is nothing wrong with the sense of pride generated by owning your own business. Building your ego can be very beneficial, but there is a big difference between ego and egotistical.

6. Satisfaction? There is nothing more satisfying than reaping what you sow. Starting a business is difficult, and more hard work than you have probably ever done. But, when your company becomes profitable, there is no greater feeling than the satisfaction you feel looking at that which you have built with your own sweat and determination.

7. Money? Although looked down upon by some as a reason, money is the mother's milk of business. A business without money is a business

that will starve to death, and it could financially cripple you as well. No one starts a business to fill the pockets of their vendors. Unless you are doing volunteer work, we are all in it for the money. From the fast food employee to the Chairman of the Board, we work for others…or for ourselves…for money. Money is a tremendous motivator because of what can be done with it once it is possessed. Money is necessary to put food on the table, provide for our retirement, and everything in between. Money drives people to succeed, instead of staying home to watch the next television program.

8. Want to be a millionaire? Few people don't, and more people join this group everyday. It is a goal that you may want to attempt someday, but never forget the first goal when you start a business…getting your business to support itself. If your business can't support itself, it will never support you, and you will never reach your long term goal of hitting that first million. You will also need to know the limitations of your business. If you are a one person cleaning service, you can provide a nice living for yourself and your family, but becoming a millionaire will never happen…at least not as a result of owning your own business. To reach that goal, you would have to undertake other activities, such as hiring employees, adding locations, branching out into new cities, possibly even franchising. Any of these will add it's own new set of opportunities and problems.

9. Want to rub your former employer's nose in it? If you and your former employer parted on less than the best terms, this can be a strong motivator. You would need to stay in the same industry, and become a competitor to your former employer for this to work. It is bad business, however, to make this an open goal. Keep this desire to yourself, and don't talk ill of your former employer as you speak to customers. Let your success do the talking for you. Being successful will do more to drive your former boss crazy than anything you could say to him or her.

10. Tired of just making ends meet? The frustration factor of making just enough money to pay the bills is a strong motivation. By itself, though, it's not enough motivation to make a business successful. There is nothing more frustrating than the sacrifices you have to make when starting a business. It may be a long time before the business is successful enough to support you. If you leave your steady paycheck behind, you will have to be prepared for the possibility of going without any income for quite some time. You must be willing to accept the short term sacrifices for the long term goal.

11. Tired of seeing others profit from your ideas and hard work? Many who have the entrepreneurial spirit get tired of seeing the profits of their labor line the pockets of their employer, even though that is what they are paid to do. When you work for someone else, you trade the profit and the risk for a stable paycheck. But, profit and risk are inseparable. If you decide you wish to gain all of the profits from your labor, then you have to accept all of the risk as well.

Needless to say, the reasons for starting a business are as numerous as the people that have started a business. Make sure to list your own personal reasons for wanting to start your own business.

As with many things, if there are reasons for doing something, then there are also reasons to not do something. You've listed the reasons to start a business on your sheet of paper. Now, draw a line down the center of the paper, and, on the other side, list the reasons for not starting a business. Below I have listed the most common reasons, but be sure to list your own as well.

1. Too much risk.

2. Too little money. You need to be able to hold out until your business becomes profitable.

3. Too much work. A forty-hour week will be a distant memory.

4. Too much stress.

5. No home office to blame when things go wrong.

6. No one on whom you may off-load a tough decision.

7. Too much stress on my family. If you are married and/or have children, they will be coming along for the ride when you start your business. You need to make sure your spouse is as committed to your venture as you are. This won't eliminate all of the problems, but it will make it smoother.

8. Too many details. Being an owner means never having to say "That's not my job". Everything is your job…vendors, supplies, taxes, payroll, utilities, phones, charities, advertising, hiring, firing, government compliance, inventory, customer service, shipping, warehousing, billing, banking, correspondence, janitor, computer specialist, sales, sales support…and the list goes on and on ad-nauseum.

Having completed your lists of why you should and why you shouldn't start your own business, set it to the side. You will need the list again later. Title the lists "Chapter 1". As we go through the remaining chapters, you will be asked to do similar exercises. After we are done, it will be time to examine all of this information, and for you to make the final decision…whether or not to start your own business. Working for yourself can be the most exciting, challenging, frightening, satisfying, nauseating, satisfying, and any other-ing you can ever possibly imagine. But make no mistake it is a decision to be taken seriously and not on a lark. For in addition to all the other–ings of which you think it will also be the most unforgi**ving**, and bankrupt**ing**, if you aren't properly prepared and determined. Each and every year more than 45,000 businesses close their doors. That's the end of a dream for more than 45,000 business owners every year. Owners who were excited and exuberant the day their doors opened, yet were forced to watch their dreams fall apart before their eyes. Don't risk your savings and security on a lark. Don't start a business because you think it would be a fun thing to do. It can be fun, but only if you have the determination to make it work. If you don't, I can promise you it won't be fun for very long.

Still with me? You haven't thrown the book on the floor and run away screaming yet? Maybe you should have your head examined…are you nuts?…are you crazy? (The combination comments are always classics.)

You're still here??? Turn the page…Chapter 1 is done…time to move on with your life…well…okay, I give up…I'm going on to Chapter 2 whether you come with me or not.

I'm gone…really I am…I hate this, seeing who will turn the page first. I have an idea…"I'll race you to Chapter 2…get ready….get set…

Chapter Two

▼

Preparation

Go! I never said I'd play fair…but I did beat you to Chapter 2, so there! Maybe after reading this chapter on preparation, you'll be more prepared for turning to Chapter 3. I'll see you at the end of the chapter, so pay attention; there may be a quiz. (It always worked in high school anyway.)

Before you begin to worry about the mechanics of getting your business started, there are a number of things you must do to prepare yourself mentally and financially before taking that final leap.

Financial Preparation: You will need to take a long, serious look at your current financial status. This exercise will be to determine how long you can hold out without an income. This will be the length of rope you have before you end up hanging yourself. It is critical to know how long you can go without a paycheck. Some businesses take a long time to build, others are quick starts. The more complicated, the more elaborate, the more global the business you are starting, the longer it can take to hit that glorious day of breaking even. Your business may have the greatest potential in the world, but if you run out of money before it starts generating a profit, you will be forced to abandon it…possibly on the brink of it's success.

Either copy to a sheet of paper or write on the worksheet below:

- Cash in Savings ...._____
- Cash in Checking ...._____
- Amount in Liquid Investments ...._____
  (stocks, CD's, mutual funds, bonds, etc.)
- Income from non-liquid assets ...._____/year
  (any investments you can't liquidate in the next 12 months)
- Dollar amount left on all credit cards ...._____
- Amount of equity in your home ...._____
- Annual after-tax income of your spouse ...._____
  TOTAL ...._____

This is the amount of money to which you have access, without going outside to family, friends, banks, or investors.

Now you will need to calculate your monthly expenditures. The most realistic way to do this is to go through your checkbook. Open your check register for the last full year. Make sure to include 12 full months. Add together all of your spending for the last 12 months…this should include necessities, luxuries, blown money, ATM withdrawals, everything! Enter that amount below:

- Total spending for the last 12 months_____
  Now divide that number by 12:
- Average spending per month over the last year_____

You can make changes in your budget to tighten your belt, but when calculating how long you can last, it is best to use this figure as a worst case scenario. Now comes the moment of truth. Take your total accessible cash and divide by your average monthly spending:

Total Accessible Cash _____divided by average monthly spending _____ = number of months you can survive without a paycheck_____.

EXAMPLE:

If you have access to *$68,000* and you divide by your average monthly spending of *$3,500*, then you will be able to hold out for a total of *19 months*.

So…are you gasping for breath, or are you feeling confident that you can make it? (Whispers to the gaspers) "Don't worry…the confident folks should be gasping too…there are no guarantees when starting a business, no matter how much money with which you have to start."

You have now established your base line. This establishes the time by which your business must be profitable. You may ask "If the example above is for 19 months, why did I only figure 12 months worth of income from my spouse?" I guarantee you something will come up from time to time to siphon off those additional funds. This figure of 19 months takes only your family expenditures into account. Based on the above example, for every $3,500 you must put into your business, you will have to deduct 1 month from the length of time you can hold out.

Now you need to calculate how much your family will fall short each month. This will establish what you will need to be able to draw out of your business as your business becomes profitable.

- Monthly after-tax income of spouse   _____
- Monthly income from non-liquid assets   _____
- Total monthly income   _____
- Average monthly expenditures over last 12 months_____
- [Total monthly income]-[Total monthly expenditures]=_____

EXAMPLE:

Income: $1,800/month-Expenditures: $3,500/month = ($1,700)/month shortfall

Now you know how much you will need to be able to draw, and when you will have to be able to draw those funds from your new business.

Always remember and follow…in order…the steps to growing a profitable business:

♦ Phase 1: Get your business to the point where it supports itself.
♦ Phase 2: Get your business to the point where you are not going into the hole each month on your personal expenditures.
♦ Phase 3: Get your business to the point where it is generating a healthy profit that allows itself and you to thrive.

If you skip Phase 1 and go directly to Phase 2, you will most likely starve your business to death. If you want your business to support you in the long run, then you will have to leave the money it generates alone until it supports itself. ALWAYS REMEMBER: if it doesn't support itself, it won't support you for long.

Now you know how long you can hold out. Next, you need to know in what order to source the money. Keep in mind that credit cards are always the last place to go to get the cash you need to survive.

• First Source of Funds—Assets you can liquidate are your first source of funds. Savings, CD's, stocks, mutual funds, etc.; any source of funds that you can liquidate without incurring a penalty. If cashing in your CD, mutual fund, bond, etc., would result in a penalty, move that source to the secondary source of funds. If you are hesitant about liquidating one of these assets, you shouldn't be. You will pay a higher interest rate on borrowed money than you will receive on invested money. As a result, it will be cheaper in the long run for you to liquidate these funds first. Also, if you have an automatic withdrawal set up for your checking account to fund a retirement account, stop it immediately. That cash will be more beneficial to you now to minimize the amount you are going into the hole each month.

• Second Source of Funds—If you have CD's and mutual funds, and would incur a penalty to liquidate, cash them as they mature. A retirement account will carry with it a tax penalty for liquidating the account. If your business becomes profitable within a year, you will be money ahead to pull the funds you need from a credit card, compared against the penalties for liquidating that retirement account. If your business takes longer than a year to become profitable, you will be money ahead by paying the tax penalty and liquidating the account. Another source of funds will be the equity in your home. Don't start looking for borrowed money until you have exhausted your liquid assets. The benefit with the home equity loan is that they are also often tax deductible.

- Third Source of Funds—Now is the time to start hitting those credit cards. But, before you start hitting the bank for those cash advances, call your credit card company and find out if they offer credit card checks. Many credit card companies offer a lower interest rate on the checks than the card. But, before you think the credit card company is being generous, you have to look at the purpose for offering the checks and the lower interest rate. These checks give the credit card companies access to businesses that don't accept credit cards. The credit card company can now get interest on purchases for items such as your electric bill, your mortgage, etc. But, by giving you the ability to pay for bills with these credit card checks, you can eliminate the need for cash advances. If you are going into the hole $1,500 a month, don't go to the bank for a $1,500 cash advance. On a cash advance, you pay a fee of up to 1 month of interest to get the cash advance. In addition, you start paying interest the day you obtain the cash advance. If you are able to obtain the credit card checks, then pay $1,500 worth of bills with the checks. With the checks, you will not be paying the 1 month interest cash advance fee, and quite often you won't begin to accumulate interest until the next billing cycle.

As the debt on your credit cards rises, you may want to look into consolidation loans. A consolidation loan will allow you to stretch the length of time you can hold out, and will often save you 2 or 3 points of interest compared to your credit cards. Be on your guard however, there are many companies that offer consolidation loans. Most are legitimate, but many will gouge you if you give them the opportunity. Never pursue a consolidation loan from a company that charges any up front fees. These fees will often make the load more expensive than your credit card interest rates. Also, there are several disreputable loan companies that will insist on an application fee, and will not refund the money once you are declined. These companies are in the business of declining people, and are interested in little more than screwing you out of an application fee. So, I cannot stress enough...PAY NO UP FRONT FEES, NO APPLICATION FEES, AND NO CLOSING FEES. There are companies that will disguise these fees as closing costs. Even though they call it a home equity loan, it is simply a consolidation loan, and you would be hard pressed getting the interest deductions past the IRS if audited. This loan is often unsecured, and won't be attached to your house. If the loan isn't attached to your house, it's not a home equity loan, and therefore, won't have closing costs. This is simply a gimmick to get you to pay an up front fee. There are many reputable companies, so look for the ones that don't assess these up front charges. Let's look at an example involving a fictitious consolidation loan company:

Scheister, Cheatya, and Takeya Consolidation Loan Company

They receive a $59 application fee, $2,200 in closing costs, and an interest rate of 15% on a $20,000 loan. In actuality you are paying 11.3% interest up front, so you are paying a total of 26% interest on that $20,000. These companies do loan sharks proud, so stay away from them.

Additional Sources of funds:

I. *Family and Friends*-Make sure they understand the money is at risk, and that if your business would fail, they won't disown you. If a friend loans you money, and your business goes in the toilet, you may lose a friend. Your family may not be able to change your name to 'The relative formerly known as son', but life could become interesting around the holidays if that money is never coming back. So, ask them about a million or so times "Are you sure? You won't have me hunted by Uncle Fester…or lock me in a room with all of my nieces and nephews…or make me sit at the kids table at Thanksgiving?" before accepting that check.

II. *SBA Guaranteed Loan*-This can be a difficult proposition. To get an SBA loan, you have to first be approved for the loan by a bank. They will send your loan to the SBA to be guaranteed, and you will pay an insurance fee to the SBA for the guarantee. If you decide to try for an SBA guaranteed bank loan, have the loan proposal written by an accountant. Bankers have a specific way in which they like to see projections and numbers on a page. Present the proposal in a way other than what they want, and I promise your proposal will never be given the slightest consideration. Every banker has their own way that they like to view assumptions, business plans, etc. You will be time and money ahead working with an accountant who knows the banks and how they like to see the material presented. Once you find an accountant that can help you, be persistent. A good accountant can work wonders with your business plan, but they can't perform miracles. You will repeatedly hear "Not in business long enough", or "Not enough capital to secure the loan", before you get to a "Yes". Always check with the SBA on special programs that are available. If you are a woman or a government recognized minority, often there are programs to relax the standards the banks use in judging loan requests. In addition, as a woman or government recognized minority, the SBA may have money of their own available. The SBA will often target segments of the business community to boost female and minority involvement, so check with them for an update. Just remember, use

every opportunity to your advantage. If they are looking for women
with agoraphobia…wearing pink…who will only sing on Tuesdays
when the moon is full…carrying a poodle in a polka-dot
sweater…hopping on one leg…I suggest you warm up that voice and
get ready for the next full moon. Making your business successful is
what matters, and if the government has a program that will help you,
then use it to your full advantage. Don't worry about whether or not
a program is 'fair' by not being available to everyone. The government
is one of the most unfair entities that exist today. The success of your
business will be good for the economy and the country. Our economy
isn't a giant single monolith; it is composed of thousands upon thousands of small components…your business being one. The ripple
effect each of those has can be good or bad. When your business is
good, the ripples of your activity are felt long and far. You buy a sta-
pler, which helps the store you purchased it from, the wholesaler that
sold it to the store, the manufacturer, and the families of all three of
those, who then buy goods from other stores, etc. The ripples go on
and on in an ever expanding circle. When your business fails, those
ripples are still felt by the absence of your purchases. A good axiom to
keep in mind is that your vendors will always miss you more than
your customers will when your business fails. This relates to your
business as well. You would miss your customer much more than you
would miss one of your vendors. A customer will always find someone to fill the need, whether your business exists or not, but your
business can't exist without its customers. So…if you learn nothing
else…you should learn this…here it comes…get your pen ready for a
goodie…all set????? "YOUR CUSTOMER CAN EXIST WITH-
OUT YOU, BUT YOUR BUSINESS CAN'T EXIST WITHOUT
ITS CUSTOMERS." So, keep your priorities straight and hold onto
those customers with all your life. Have I digressed long enough? all
right already…now…where was I? Oh yeah…#3…sorry…I'll be
quiet…Oooooooohhh…Investors…looks interesting…

III. *Investors*-To do this so that you're not in violation of Federal Securities laws, you will need to do a few things before actively seeking investors.

 A. First, you will need to incorporate. An S Corporation will most likely be the best for you. The business will pay no taxes. The tax liability will flow straight to the shareholder(s) so you will only pay taxes once. With a S Corporation, however, other companies cannot invest in your business; only individuals.

 B. Get a corporate attorney and tell him what you are planning to do. Your attorney will be able to supply you with the disclosure forms you will need for investors to sign, so that you will be in compliance with the securities laws. I'm not spending a great deal of time discussing what compliance involves because compliance varies from state to state. If you are going to sell securities in other states check with your attorney. According to how you are conducting the sale you may be required to register your securities in each state in which they will be sold.

 C. If you are filed as a S Corporation do not advertise in the newspaper or any other media. This is against securities laws, and can get you into a lot of trouble. Again, check with your attorney to find out how you can legally promote the sale of shares within your state.

IV. *Partners*-If you have a specific vision for your business and a well-defined view of what you want to accomplish, this option should be considered a last resort. Having a partner or partners can allow more work to be done and the expense of starting a business to be diluted across more people, but you give up the autonomy and the single focus and vision you have for your company. If you have multiple partners, you will then run the risk of your vision becoming lost to the majority. No one can force you to sell your shares in the company, but if there is a dispute among the partners, you could be fired by the other partners, and forced to leave the business you started. So think carefully about bringing partners into your business. They can be a blessing or a curse, but often are not worth the headaches they create. The exception to this, of course, is if you can retain 50% + 1 share or more of your company. If you can bring partners on board under that condition, you will be able to retain control and maintain the vision you have for your company. This will allow you to gather input and opinions from your other partners, but retain the ability to make the final decision yourself. If you decide to bring partners into your company define everything. It may sound like too much of a headache, but it will stop many disputes from arising. If your partners are your friends this becomes even more paramount. Friends will assume far too much with regard to one another for a partnership to survive. Friends will tend to not put many agreed decisions in writing. Why should they? They're friends after all, aren't they? You will be amazed how fast friendship can fly out the window when money is involved. You will also be amazed how forgetful they can be about past decisions once money becomes a dividing issue. Stop the conflicts before they start by putting every decision in writing, and every partner signing off on each and every decision. You will also need to agree on perceptions and procedures. Let me put forth an example of what I mean by using a hypothetical situation. You have started a company and brought two of your friends in as partners. Your two partners charge their expenses to the company. You charge your expenses to your own credit cards and then write an expense check to yourself. For ease of the example we will say each partner spent $1,000. Your two partners charged $1,000 each to the company. You paid the $1,000 and then wrote an expense check to yourself for $1,000. The company has paid $1,000 worth of expenses for each partner. Your two partners however, are up in arms because you wrote an expense check to yourself. Logically there is no difference.

The company paid $1,000 per partner. All your partners see however, is a check written to you, and no amount of logic can convince them that you aren't getting more of the pie than are they. This is a dispute that could be avoided by simply agreeing ahead of time how expenses are to be handled. Another huge point of contention between partners is workload. Some people, especially if they have never before owned a business, can become what I call *professional owners*. As an employee these are people that think owners do little other than attend social functions, golf with customers, and do the *'big deal'*. Often one partner will work himself to death trying to sell enough product to keep up with the company expenditures, and the spending habits of his partners. This can create a strain on the relationships of the partners as one eats at fast food drive-thrus and stays at Motel 6, while the others eat lobster, play golf, stay at $150 a night hotels, and are working on the 'big deal' that will generate phantom millions years down the road. All partners need to know that the business needs to generate money today if it is going to be around years down the road. These professional owners generate little revenue yet tend to have large expenses. All of the partners need to agree up front how expenses will be permitted and workload distributed. Cash is always tight when you start a business. There is nothing wrong with setting caps on expenditures such as food, hotels, entertaining, etc. Once the caps are in place it will eliminate a point of possible contention. If the limit on a dinner is $10 and your partner wants to spend $50 on a lobster dinner it will no longer be a big deal, because $40 of the bill is at his own expense. These examples all boil down to one thing; no detail is too small when working out agreements with partners ahead of time. Starting a business is hard enough without adding internal difficulties through strained partner relationships.

V. *Other Sources for Minor Funds-*

    A. You can get a part time job to help extend the length of time your money will last.

    B. Try to get terms longer than 30 days from your vendors. Many will work with you starting out. They want new customers just as you do, and are willing to help to insure that you will stay in business and grow as customers of their business.

    C. If your business generates invoices to receive payment, invoice fast. The normal term you offer a customer is 30 days. Try to get them to pay quicker by offering a 1% discount if paid in 10 days. This will get your money into you quickly, and if you are able to get longer terms from your vendors, this allows you to operate on the vendor's money for a period of time.

Many of the exercises done thus far have been to establish your financial boundaries, but also to help you mentally prepare for the challenge you are getting ready to face. The mental preparation necessary to undergo the starting of a business is as, if not more, important than any other preparation you undertake. In starting a new business, you will be undertaking one of the greatest challenges of your life. Eighty percent of new businesses fail within the first year. You must ask why they fail. The reasons for a business failing are many. Let's take some time to examine some of the most common:

- *Reason#1*-Lack of commitment. Many people have the emotional enthusiasm that is present at the start of a business. Reality, however, is a rude teacher, and when it hits each new business owner full in the face, many fold to the pressure and close their business. Starting a business is not easy; if it were, there would only be employers, no employees. When the difficulties begin, you must be determined to stick with it until you and your business are financially stable.

Determination must be the word you live by when starting a business. If you don't make a sale, you pick yourself up and go again the next day, and the next, and the next. Knowing the number of months you can hold on will give you the focus you need to succeed. Therefore, don't be discouraged if you don't reach your goal of breaking even the first, second, third month, etc. Keep focused on your goal and strive every day to reach it, no matter the obstacles you face.

- *Reason #2*-Money. Many new businesses start out under-capitalized. They struggle from day one. I speak of this category from personal experience. Of all the businesses I have owned or started over the years, not one has been properly capitalized at the time of start up. An under-capitalized business can become successful, but it takes a tremendous amount of work, and often funding from your own pocket to nurse it through it's infancy. Starting an under-capitalized business takes an extraordinary commitment to see the business through. Starting without the resources to make a splash in the market, your business will tend to take longer to develop than businesses with the proper resources behind them. Unfortunately, for many starting their own business, getting the money to properly capitalize a business before you start it is next to impossible. If you are going to start your business under-capitalized, you must go in with your eyes open, and ready for the struggle you are preparing to undertake. But, always remember…you must risk greatly to succeed greatly.

- *Reason #3*-Lousy idea. Sometimes it's just the simple fact that you start a business that holds no interest to the customers. Make sure you've taken a hard enough look at your product or service to know whether or not there exists a potential customer base. You can accomplish this by either knowing the customer base already, or doing sufficient research to discover the answers before you take the plunge.

- *Reason #4*-No expertise. It never pays to start or purchase a business about which you know nothing and have no experience. If you want to buy or start a retail shop, work in retail for a few months; learn about retail sales and service. If it's a restaurant, get experience working in a restaurant. It will be critical for you to not only have some experience and expertise, but to enjoy what you are doing. The worst situation you can put yourself in is to buy or start a business that 'sounded' good, only to discover that you hate that business. It is a recipe for failure. You will need to LOVE what you do…in the beginning that will be all you have to keep you going from day to day.

- *Reason #5*-Bad Location. There are businesses that rely to some degree on location. Here are some examples of businesses in very bad locations:

  1. A flea market in an upscale neighborhood. (Maybe the servants shop there.)

  2. A bank next to a prison. (At least the inmates don't have to go far for a withdrawal.)

  3. A fast food restaurant in the arts district. (Maybe a Picasso burger would have done the trick.)

  4. A gas station on a corner that renders it inaccessible from three directions and nearly impossible to exit. (They'll need to re-fill before getting out of the lot.)

  5. A discount department store two miles out of town, by itself, and surrounded by a corn field. (At least they had no competition)

  6. A corn seed company in Florida, trying to sell seed in the midwest. (Customers may have been 1,000 miles away, but think of the tan.)

  7. A taxi company in a small, rural town. (A job going nowhere.)

8. A housing development that was split down the middle by very active railroad tracks. (Living there would have been a 'moving' experience.)

9. An adult bookstore next door to a church. (They were doomed and damned at the same time.)

10. A drive-in movie theater next to an airport. (If they would only time the departures with the on-screen earthquake effects.)

So make sure your location will serve your customers well, so that your business will serve you well.

• ***Reason #6***-Mismanagement. You must be able to track where your money goes and from where it comes. Being able to track accurately isn't only for tax purposes. If you don't track properly, your business can get away from you before you realize how much money has disappeared.

Whatever the specific reason for a business failure, it usually falls into one of the above six categories. If you want your business to be a member of the 20% Club of successful start-ups, you must be prepared…and you must be determined.

Okay…that's the end of the chapter…ready to go on to Chapter 3? Still want to take the risk of starting that business?…Let's take a look now….and see if your family is ready to take the plunge with you…

CHAPTER THREE

▼

FAMILY

It is impossible to emphasize too greatly the importance of your family being behind you in your new venture. Money is the biggest cause of arguments and discord between a husband and wife. Starting a business will amplify the money arguments many fold. It is imperative, therefore, that your spouse know and understand the potential hardships that are coming during the start-up phase of your business.

You must understand that divorce is a real possibility for the person who doesn't involve their spouse from the moment the idea to start a business enters your head. Keeping your spouse involved and informed will, however, help your marriage to survive the hardships you may endure.

This chapter is dedicated to keeping your family relationships strong so that when you begin to reap the rewards of owning your own business, you haven't sacrificed the most important thing of all in your journey...your family.

Your relationship with your spouse will have a tremendous bearing on your business, children, and every aspect of your life. From the beginning, talk to your spouse about your ideas, dreams, and why you want to start your own business. If your spouse opposes the idea, listen to his/her reasons; they are most likely well-founded. Starting a business can be a very scary thing to do. You will be putting your entire family at risk along with you, so make sure your spouse can accept that risk. Involve your spouse in the planning of your new business. Seek advice and talk to your spouse in realistic terms of what your family may have to endure. Don't speak only of blue skies and riches to your spouse. If you do this, you will simply be trying to fool your spouse, and maybe yourself, into believing it will be easy. If starting a new business was easy, nearly 80% of them wouldn't fail each year.

You may not be able to convince your spouse to be enthusiastic about your new venture. In that case, all you can hope for is that, although not excited, your spouse will support your decision. If, however, your spouse is utterly opposed to the idea, proceeding forward anyway is a very bad idea. If you are determined to own your own business, continue to try to sway your spouse, but don't go forward until you can at least get some sort of agreement of support from your spouse. To proceed anyway, against the wishes of your spouse, will do nothing but create conflict and hard feelings within your home.

Once your spouse decides to support your decision, don't think for a second the battle has been won and life will be a bed of roses. Now is the time you will need to be as focused on your family as you are on your new business.

Before your new business, you and your spouse may have enjoyed all sorts of activities together. Most likely every one of them cost money; shopping, theater, movies, dining out, ballet, sports games, etc…the list may be quite extensive. Unless you've started your business loaded with enough cash to survive the start-up phase with no change in lifestyle, you will have to give up a lot of activities that require money.

So, since you have to cut back on activities, does that mean the two of you should just sit around and stare at each other or the television everyday? I guarantee if you do, there will be trouble ahead at home.

You will need to be inventive in coming up with things that cost little or nothing at all…yet will continue to provide the activity and attention that are necessary for a relationship to thrive. Here are a few ideas to make sure that the flame keeps burning…even when reality hits you like a fire hose:

* Love notes left in the car or throughout the house.

* Go for walks together.

* Pampering nights-drop off the kids at grandma and grandpa's, and have a romantic dinner at home, a little dancing in the living room, maybe a bubble bath for two, and let nature take it's course.

* Contact a seed elevator in your area. You can buy 50 to 60 pounds of corn for $5 or $6. Then take your spouse and your children to feed the ducks and geese at a local park or public lake. A bushel of corn can last you all summer and provide a lot of fun for the family, not to mention how much the ducks and geese will enjoy the treat.

* Watch the kids for a day. Either take the kids somewhere so you spouse can have an empty house for the day, or kick your spouse out of the house to go do something enjoyable…while you take care of the kids at home.

* Take care of all the household duties for your spouse for a day. Make it your 'king' or 'queen' day, and wait on them hand and foot.

* Write out coupons to give to your spouse. They can involve household duties, favors, child duty, a massage, and that (censored) thing you can do that you know your spouse absolutely loves. Now, once the coupons are written and delivered, be ready to honor them whenever your spouse chooses…whether you are in the mood to perform the activity or not.

Be inventive; it's not the money you spend with or on your spouse that keeps the love burning, it's the effort you put into the relationship that acts as the mortar as you continue to build your relationship.

Your children…unless you and your spouse fight about your financial difficulties while building your business…will be oblivious to the financial hardships you may have to endure. How the children perceive their situation will be entirely dependent on you and your spouse. Here are some of the guidelines you should follow to protect your children from whatever stress or storm comes upon you while starting your business:

- Don't take any personal frustrations out on your children. Blowing up at your children, using them as a release valve, is not why God put them on this earth.

- If you and your spouse feel that you simply must fight, do it away from the children. Few things will hurt a child more than seeing or hearing their parents yelling at each other. Fighting in another room isn't good enough. Few homes are so soundproof that the children won't be able to hear you fighting. Another benefit to 'scheduled' fights is that by the time the kids are away and the two of you are alone and free to fight, you may have cooled off and not even feel like fighting anymore.

- Take your kids to cheap or free activities:
  a) a public playground
  b) feeding the ducks and geese
  c) buy an annual pass to the zoo or children's museum. It provides for you the opportunity of going as many times as you wish. It's very economical since often the annual fee is often recouped after 2 or 3 visits.

- Go to a public park, play ball, wrestle, picnic, throw a Frisbee, whatever your family enjoys…just enjoy it together.

Take care not to lose sight of your child while starting your business. It is very easy to immerse yourself in your new venture, and spend less and less time with your children. Your children only live with you a short while, and then they are gone. The most precious moments with your children only happen once. They only take their first step one time, say their first word one time, go to the first day of school one time, learn to ride a bike one time, have their first crush one time, their first heartbreak one time, their first prom one time, their first driver's license one time. And, if you are to absorbed in starting your new business venture to have all of those wonderful 'one time' memories, before you know it they will be gone, and you will wonder where the time went and how you missed seeing your children grow up.

Sacrifice-Most likely you will need to make some sacrifices to extend the length of time your money will last until your business becomes profitable. You will need to take a look at every expenditure you family has, and figure out how to squeeze every penny of savings out of your budget:

- Less movies…or wait until the movie you want to see hits the dollar theater.

- Less dining out.

- Stop payments to your mutual fund or IRA until your business becomes profitable.

- Less of the expensive junk food and snacks in the house.

- Hold on to your clothes until they wear out, not just until they go out of fashion.

- Donate some of your unwanted things to a charity. The tax deduction is as good as cash.

- Work a part time job.

- Start your business part time (if possible), and work a full time job until your business income can replace your salary.

- Drop magazine subscriptions (except trade magazines).

- Buy based on need, not on want.

Every month you will need to squeeze and squeeze until there isn't another penny to be squeezed from your budget. I know sacrifice is never fun. There will be times when you just want to pitch it all and go back to the way you used to live. Just don't forget that what you are striving for is worth the sacrifice. You don't get rich working for someone else unless you play professional sports or are a politician; working for yourself will involve a time of 'paying your dues'.

Insurance-Health and life insurance are critical for your family while your are self-employed. I hope the reason for health insurance is self-evident. If something catastrophic happened, it would most likely bankrupt you, and, as a result, bankrupt your business. Life insurance is an 'absolute…no question…don't dare start a business without it' must. You and your spouse must have a large amount on each other. If your spouse were to die, you would need to find child-care for your children while you are working. You would have much more to do around the house, and may be forced to hire a service to assist you with the household duties. You will have the expense of the funeral, and with the emotional difficulties of losing a spouse, the last thing you need is financial difficulty as well. Make sure that there is enough insurance on your spouse to hire help around the house, pay off any debts you have, including the mortgage, pay for the funeral, and supply you with enough money on which to live for a period of 3 to 5 years…as a cushion.

You should have even more insurance on yourself. The reasons are the same as above, with some additions. Your spouse will have to either take over your business, sell your business, or close your business. All three of these choices will have their own unique expenses. I would recommend your spouse either sell or close the business, and not try to take it over. If they are not involved with managing it on a daily basis, the business could become a financial 'black hole'. Make sure your spouse understands that if you were to die, he/she shouldn't try to continue it out of loyalty to you and your memory. The first duty of your spouse will be to take care of her/him self and your children. I feel it is best to carry enough insurance that when invested in a safe fund, will be enough to support the family without it being necessary for the spouse to work.

Don't spend your money on whole life or any dividend-paying policies. You need your cash for your survival and these plans are expensive. Simply get a good term policy from a reputable insurance carrier and agent. By the time the term expires, your business should be profitable and, if you so choose, you can then move to the more expensive policies.

Vacations-While you are building your business, Las Vegas, Disney World, or the Bahamas may be out of the question, but the need to get away will still be there. Make sure you create time to get away, even if only for the weekend. Rent a cabin somewhere, go to an amusement park, something...anything. Don't get so wrapped up that you ignore the need of your family and yourself to wave it all good-bye and get away for a few days now and then. You will be amazed how much more refreshed and mentally recharged you will be after some time away. You will get more done as well.

Three chapters down and still preparing...well...guess what?...we're still preparing in chapter four, so keep on reading...and hopefully one day you'll actually get to read about starting that business you're so all fired up about...

▼

FOCUS, NAMING, AND FILING STATUS

You have the desire to own your own business, the determination to make it work, and your family is behind you. You have it made! But…what in the world is your business going to do? What makes it different? Why should a customer choose you over a competitor? What is your niche? What is your focus? This you must decide before the door ever opens or your phone ever rings. What makes your company 'your company'? Do you take the shotgun approach and get into a little bit of everything hoping something will stick? Do you concentrate on one thing and do it the best of anyone? The answer is yes to both and no to both. But, before you get to that stage, how do you decide what your business is going to do? Maybe you don't even have an idea of what to do. Whether you decide to start a business, buy an existing business, or buy a franchise, you must know the advantages and limitations of each, and then make the decision of what business to enter. Let's take them one at a time…okay?

Starting a Business from Scratch:

This method of getting into business is very exciting and satisfying when it is successful. This method also has the highest failure rate, primarily due to the fact that most people just don't know what they have gotten themselves into until it's too late. Under-prepared and under-capitalized are the two main reasons for these failures. This category takes the entrepreneur with the most vivid imagination. Every aspect of your business must come from your own head. You must set yourself apart from your competitors. To do that, you must know your competitors better than they know themselves. The point I'm making here is that to start a business from scratch you must have expertise in the business, whatever it may be. You cannot start a business from scratch that you know nothing about; it will be doomed to failure because you will not be able to anticipate the problems and pitfalls that are sure to befall you. You must ask yourself what you are good at…or better at…than most others. We all have talents, even if you can't think of any. At one of our seminars, a woman in the audience raised her hand and told me jokingly, "All I'm good at is shopping." She thought she was being humorous, but she really believed she had no skills with which she could start her own business. I asked her "So just how good are you at shopping?" I asked her to come to the stage and evaluate the quality of the suit I was wearing. I also posed as a clerk in a store and had her tell me what she liked and didn't like about the way I waited on her. I drew on the overhead a store layout, and had her evaluate the accessibility of the goods, dressing rooms, checkout counters, etc. As it turned out, she was a VERY good shopper. I then suggested she should focus those skills, and as she went shopping for the next several months, write reports on her findings so that she could practice the art of critical review. I also suggested that while she was practicing, she should take a course in report writing. Upon gaining confidence in her reporting skills, she could then harness those skills into creating her own business as a critical shopper. She is now hired by store chains to go in and evaluate personnel, store layout, accessibility, competitive pricing, etc. The point is, she felt she had no talent and that is always false. We all have talents; the challenge is in identifying those talents and turning them into a profitable business. It must be something you enjoy as well. If you do not enjoy your new business, you will not last long in it.

Ready to pull out another sheet of paper? Remember to label this sheet Chapter 4-What I'm Good At. Now, what you will need to do is list all the things you are good at doing, no matter how trivial. I must specify, however, we are discussing legal activities, so no funny stuff. If you say you're good at eating, don't laugh…many food, wine, and beverage companies employ or contract professional tasters and tasting companies. But, you had better have a very discriminating palate. If you're a guy though keep in mind, a job clicking remotes to test button endurance are usually held by robots. There is little that cannot, with some creative thinking…be turned into a profitable business.

As soon as you have exhausted your brain figuring out what it is you do well, you will have to figure out how to convert that into a business. To do that you will need to identify who your potential customers might be. Let's use our shopping example: The customers are obvious…business owners or managers of retail establishments. What would be the reason they would hire our shopping service? The answer is to improve the competitiveness of their store over that of their competitors.

Everyone wants an edge over their competitor. How can our service give them that edge? You help them to improve the layout of the store so that it is more accessible and customer friendly. You help their employees to be more effective salespeople, improve their customer service. This part may require some good acting skills. The woman in this example will go into a store…being difficult and really hard on the employees to see how they handle 'pain in the you know what' customers. It seems harsh at times, but it is a rare salesclerk that will not have to face an abusive customer at some point. Being able to teach them how to do that can be an important sales tool. How easy is it to pay for the goods? The store may only accept MasterCard and Visa. Well, it's no harder for the store to accept American Express, Discover, or any other card available, so why not make paying as easy and convenient as possible for the customer. A comparison against some of the businesses in your potential customer pool may be desired…which would involve evaluating their competitors on their behalf. This can prove beneficial because when an employee of the business does this, it is hard to eliminate prejudices against the competitor. This service can be very involved and go from a one-time evaluation to a year-long study to capture the seasonal effects on the business. The point here is that you must anticipate every possible benefit to your customer. Remember, it will be your job to convince the customer to deal with you. It is not the customer's job to figure out why he should patronize your business over that of another.

You now need to decide how broad or narrow will be the focus of your business. The type of business you start will have a big effect on this focus. A restaurant that only served Chicken Kiev night after night would not last long. But the restaurant could be French, Greek, Fast Food, etc. There aren't many French gourmet fast food Greek restaurants. If your business is retail, you need to decide how broad your product lines will become. Is it a kiosk in a mall? If that is the case, the product line will be tightly focused due to the limited space. If you have a lot of available space, will your business focus as a gift shop, card shop, clothing store, etc.?

The focus you are looking for is two-fold; clothing store would be the primary focus. Your secondary focus would then be…women's?…men's?….or both…?…or children's?…teen's?…used? …conservative?…formal?…low end?…etc. The focus can continue to be defined down until you have reached the level that will fit your situation. Starting out, you will need to be narrowly enough focused so that you can handle the work that must be done, but keeping the focus broad enough to give the customer the ability to tell you what is going to hit and what will not make it in your industry. If you have focused very narrowly, by the time the market has told you that what you're doing isn't going to cut it, you may not have enough time to change your focus to something that will work.

So...to what can we boil down this entire section? Get out your pen and paper...write this down as Chapter four-Focus. The two things to remember when stating your focus:

Do something you enjoy!
Do something you are good at!

Buying an Existing Business:

The obvious benefit is that someone else has laid the groundwork and gotten the business going. Not so obvious is the fact that few people sell a successful business. Of course, when the business broker or the owner is presenting the business for your review, they will have very good reasons why they are selling. If you have looked at an existing business, you have most likely heard most of them...'more time with the family'...'retiring'...'better opportunity'...'moving'...and the list goes on and on. The reason most will not give is that the business is in trouble. When you buy a business, if you assume it is for sale because it is in trouble, you will be right almost all of the time. Don't ever trust the owner's books; they are often fiction designed for the sale. The only thing you can look at and trust will be the tax returns of the business. If you ever hear, "Forget those returns, take a look at my private books, this place is a goldmine," you're more likely going to get the shaft. It doesn't mean you can't still buy the business, but that you should go in with eyes open. Buying a business is a negotiation, and you will most likely be across the table from someone highly motivated to sell. Use that to your advantage, and see if you can get yourself a very sweet deal.

So why would you want to buy a business that is in trouble? Excellent question...I'm proud of you for asking. You may not want to go through with it at all. You must look at yourself and your character to make that decision. The ownership will have changed, but your customers will still see it as XYZ business. If they were not particularly happy with XYZ, you are going to have to win those people back to your business. Baggage to deal with is something common with an existing business. Your gain is not having to start from scratch. Your suppliers are already set, you have a customer base on which to build, your name is in the phone book, etc. The negative possibilities are bad baggage, potential problems with suppliers due to the previous ownership, reputation problems, employee loyalty, creditors that don't care that the previous owner isn't there anymore, etc. It's a trade-off you will have to examine to determine the worth of the purchase.

Buying a Franchise

The positives are obvious in buying a franchise. You are getting into a pre-packaged business, and you will be trained by people that are experts at what your business will be doing. They can help you with every potential pitfall, you have built-in suppliers and the advantage of a known name that may carry an existing customer base. Many franchises can also help you with the selection of your location by having market studies done to determine the best site in your area. You also have the advantage of community. You will have opportunities to talk with others who have franchises of your business. This networking of ideas can prove invaluable.

The disadvantages are that all this assistance does cost money. Some franchises charge a one time up-front fee. Some charge annual fees or percentages. The franchiser may require inspections, reviews of your books, ordering, etc. The depth which the franchiser will delve into your business varies with each franchise, so check them out thoroughly, and then decide how much intrusion you can accept. You will have little or no leeway in the products or services you will offer, so imagination may have to be sacrificed to some degree. So, to gain the benefit of franchising, you will have to give up some of your individuality.

Naming Your Business

A rose by any other name would smell as sweet? Not if you're talking about business names. If your business is selling roses, and the name of your business is Stinky Greens...or Manure by the Pond, the smell of your success may be foul indeed.

The name of your business can act as additional advertising if the name will convey to the customer what your business is about. When you see the name 'Joe's Transmissions', you know Joe repairs and sells transmissions, and probably isn't a florist. There are two other methods of naming your business. You can attach your name to the business. This can be done in conjunction with the informative naming method...for example: 'Mary's Cafe', or 'Watson's Hardware'. This method can also be used alone, for example: 'Harrilsons'. The third method is to come up with a catchy name that is completely non-descriptive of what business you own. A perfect example of this is Xerox. When you have a completely non-descriptive name, advertising will be a must. It will be necessary to form an attachment between what your business does and it's name. Xerox did such a good job that their name became a verb for quite some time. I would think many of us have said in the past "I need to Xerox this". The name Xerox has become interchangeable with the verb 'to photocopy'. Few of us, though, will have the resources for that kind of advertising campaign. Make sure you don't take lightly the task of naming your business. This is absolutely critical. You will be spending a long time with that name, and changing it later because you chose poorly, is difficult and expensive. Ask yourself "What is the core of my business?" Once you answer that question, build a name around that core. Decide if you want a solid, reserved name...or if you want your name to grab people when they see it or hear it. Some examples of the two styles are below (these are fictitious names...for example only):

Wilhurst Tax Accounting	or	Keep it All Tax Specialists
Norm's Body Shop	or	You Broke it, We Fix it Body Repair
Marie's Gifts	or	I Gotta Have It! Gifts & Collectibles

Once you decide on a name, try it out on some friends and family to get their reactions and feedback. You will then need to see if the name is clear to use before expending funds for signs, literature, or setting up bank accounts. Check with the US Copyright & Trademark office, and also with the Attorney General of your state. If it is clear, make sure to register your name so that it will no longer be clear for someone else to use. This will involve registering your company name with your State's Attorney General, filing a trademark application for your company logo, and attempting to copyright the name of your company. The copyright you may or may not be able to attain. That will depend on the uniqueness of your business name. You would not, for example, be able to copyright Norm's Body Shop. You could trademark a logo for Norm's Body Shop, but you can't stop another Norm who wants to open a body shop out there somewhere from being able to use his name in the naming of his business.

Now that your business is named, you will need to decide how your business will be organized. Will you be a sole proprietorship, a limited liability company, a sub-chapter S corporation, or a sub-chapter C corporation? For the purpose of this book, we will rule out the possibility of filing as a chapter C corporation. Unless you will have assets in the hundreds of thousands, or your company's stock will be publicly traded, or you are going to accept investment money from corporations, it will not make sense at the moment. As your company grows, you can always move up to a C corporation, but moving down from a C corporation is expensive and difficult.

Sole Proprietorship-This will involve the least paperwork. Simply keep good financial records. If you are going to have employees, you will need an Employer ID number from the U. S. Department of Treasury. No matter how small your business, get a good accountant. When you start your business, you won't know every form and every tax you will need to file or follow. I can assure you a good accountant will be much cheaper than the penalties that will be assessed if your business handles its paperwork incorrectly. Under a sole proprietorship, all profits or losses will flow directly to you. The advantage is that the profits of your business are only taxed one time. A C Corporation is the only status that is taxed twice; the company is taxed when it reports a profit, and you are taxed on the dividends when you receive that profit.

If you have a partner, and are going to file as a partnership, make sure to have a buy/sell agreement written by a business attorney. Don't leave undone the planning of what will happen should one of the partners die. You will also need to have an agreement as to how profits will be divided among the partners, so as to avoid future questions or conflicts. It's never a good idea to combine personal and company money, but in a sole proprietorship, as long as you have good records, it can still be done. It is simply a matter of clearly distinguishing between personal and business funds. Do not, however, use the company funds to pay personal bills. If you get audited, you will have to answer questions as to the legitimacy of your financial records. The drawback in a sole proprietorship or a partnership is liability. You will have no legal entity separating and protecting your personal assets from a liability your business may incur. Any debts, judgments, fines, penalties, etc., that are incurred by your business are attachable to your personal assets. So decide carefully; the ease of a sole proprietorship or partnership is attractive, but having no cushion between you and the business can prove disastrous to you personally…should the business fail or be hit with a large judgment or expense.

Limited Liability Company status, or LLC, is a stage between sole proprietorship and an S corporation. It offers the protection of an S corporation, which is important. If the business incurs debt, judgments, etc., the business is liable, not you. This is a wonderful protection for your personal assets. An LLC doesn't require as much paperwork in regard to meetings and decisions, but keeping personal and business funds separate becomes more critical. If you are considering filing as an LLC, contact your accountant to see if your state recognizes LLC's; not all will recognize an LLC as a legitimate status for your business.

S corporations, if done properly, offer you full protection of your personal assets. The advantages compared to a C corporation status are that profits flow straight to the shareholder(s) and are not taxed at the company level. But, with all of the advantages of protection you gain with this status, you will have to accept all of the additional paperwork that will be required of you. You will have to understand that the term 'owner' is much more ambiguous in a corporation. You will actually be a shareholder of the corporation. Keeping personal and corporate money separate is exceedingly critical with this filing status. If you don't look, act, and breathe like a corporation, a judge…or the IRS…can throw out your status as a corporation, and hold you personally liable…as if you were a sole proprietorship.

So what do I do different as a corporation, and how could I mess it up?

1. Even if you are the only shareholder, you will have to conduct shareholder meetings, meetings of the Board of Directors, elect officers, and keep minutes. I know it sounds silly to have a 'one person meeting' as a shareholder, elect yourself to the Board of Directors, elect yourself to office, and keep minutes about the decisions you make, but it is necessary. A judge will not excuse this responsibility because you feel silly. You will need to hold a Board of Directors' meeting and a shareholder meeting at least annually…even if you are the only shareholder.

2. Keep personal and corporate money separate. If you need to contribute money to the corporation so that it can pay its bills during startup, write the check to the corporation, and then have the corporation pay its bills. Do not write personal checks to pay for bills incurred by the company. An attorney coming after you will be able to show that there is no distinction between you and the company, and you will lose the protection of the corporation. As you put money into the company, make sure the company issues you a loan statement. To maintain the separation between you and the corporation, you will have to possess a promissory note showing that the corporation owes the money to you. You will also need to assign an interest rate to that money so that you will be perceived as a legitimate creditor of the corporation. You will also lose your protection if the corporation pays any of your personal bills. A

good attorney will be able to show that you don't distinguish any difference between yourself and the corporation.

3. Salary-Once the business becomes profitable, you will need to establish for yourself at least a modest salary. If you don't draw a salary, once profitable, the IRS will view you as a sole proprietorship…and revoke your corporate status.

4. Dividends-Once the business is profitable, you will need to distribute the profits. If you are the only shareholder, you will still need to vote in your corporate minutes when those dividends will be issued. Stick to the distribution schedule you voted upon in your corporate minutes. You can issue dividends annually, semi-annually, monthly, weekly; as often or seldom as you like. If you don't adhere to the distribution schedule, and you take money as you please, again you will jeopardize your status as a corporation.

Investors within an S corporation-As a corporation, your company will issue stock to its shareholders. This will enable you to seek out investors if you so choose. As an S corporation, however, there are many restrictions on how you can and cannot seek that money. Your company will have to comply with the Federal Securities and Exchange laws governing investors and stock. You must have an attorney, or you can be sure your company will leave itself open for problems in the future. As an S corporation, you cannot publicly seek funds. This means no newspaper ads or advertisements of any kind. To advertise for investors, you would have to file an IPO (Initial Public Offering) and move up to a C corporation. IPO's can be expensive to implement, costing from $20,000 to $100,000…according to the complexity involved. Once public, you could register your stock to be publicly traded on an exchange, or supervise the initial distribution yourself. Once public, however, you will have no control over the reselling of your stock. If you wish to retain control of the reselling of stock, you will need to contact your attorney to make sure it is done properly.

When you seek people to invest in your company, discuss your options with your corporate attorney. You must understand that your corporate attorney represents the corporation, not you...so make sure your attorney specifies the liability of the corporation and/or your potential personal liability when he speaks of what is legal and illegal.

Your attorney will most likely provide you with a very thick set of papers that will tell a potential investor that they could be kissing their money good-bye, and not to come crying to you if they never see that money again. Of course, when politicians and attorneys are involved, those two sentences end up being stretched to 20 pages or better. Anyone that will agree to invest in your company will need to sign the waiver provided by your attorney. As long as you follow all of your corporate by-laws, this waiver will protect you...should the investor have a complaint against the corporation someday...or if your business should fail. Also, as you seek investors, remember that another corporation cannot invest in an S corporation...only individuals. It will most likely not be necessary to name individual investors to the Board of Directors, but consult with your attorney about this matter.

Unless an investor brings some knowledge or expertise to the table that will benefit your company by their presence on the Board, don't add anyone to the Board unless necessary. Under corporate law, the Board of Directors is the entity that actually manages the corporation. It also doesn't matter how many shares each Director owns. Each Director has one vote, whether you own 1% or 99% of the company. As a result, your voice will be only one, and if the Board out-votes your proposal, the only way to override the Board of Directors is to call a shareholder meeting and call for the election of a new Board of Directors. If you have controlling interest in the company, you will be able to name yourself as the only Director, but you will most likely have very agitated investors. It is best to avoid the problem ahead of time by not adding anyone you don't have to add to the Board in the first place.

So make sure you examine each filing option carefully, and choose the organizational status that will serve you and your business best.

Okay…I'm going to hide in the corner…cringing and waiting…until you have read the title of the next chapter…so…don't hurt me….deal? Hmmmmm….no answer….I think I'll leave now…

CHAPTER FIVE

▼

GETTING STARTED

"Getting started? We're five chapters deep!!!! I've planned budgets, organized my company, got my family behind me, named my company, and you say we're just getting started?"

<Looking sheepish> "Ummmmmmmmmmm....Yes..." <Ducking for cover> But I never said it was easy. Now that all the preliminaries... <ducks, waiting to be hit>....are out of the way, we need to dive in to the fun stuff. The actual mechanics of getting your business up and running can be a lot of fun. If you enjoy playing chess or putting puzzles together, you are going to have a lot of fun putting your business together. To me, this stage is the most exciting. In the remainder of the book we will go step by step through the process of getting your company off the ground. Over the next several chapters, we will look at the tasks involved in getting businesses off the ground, and look separately at storefronts, service businesses, mail order companies, Internet companies, wholesale companies, and the roadside/festival/flea market business. So...roll up your sleeves...and let's dive into tackling a storefront.

Starting a storefront...
Are you mad????...
Are you...NUTS?!?!?!?!?!?

Are you looking for a way to lose a lot of money really, really fast????....

Now you may think that those three questions are funny, and may have even answered them quickly with a resounding "NO!". The truth, however, is that for the vast majority of people who open a storefront, the answer to the first two questions is no, but the answer to the third question is yes. Unwittingly and unintentionally yes, but yes nonetheless. Most storefronts are only open for a few short months. The sequence is repeated over and over again throughout every state in our country.

1. The owner opens his store to the public.

2. The owner exhausts his cash reserves.

3. The owner shuts the doors and goes out of business.

It is a sad cycle that you do not have to follow. The obvious question then becomes "Why?" What are the reasons that a store goes out of business? Why does a person who is confident, excited, and pumped up enough to sink their money into a venture, wait in horror as their own personal Titanic sinks beneath the waves.

Reason #1. This is the biggie, numero uno, big kahuna, beyond compare, top banana, ain't none bigger reason storefronts go out of business. ::::::drumroll::::: May I have the envelope please...?

Under Capitalization

Burn those two words deeply into your brain. Storefronts are exceedingly unforgiving to people who are under capitalized. Take a walk through your local mall sometime if you doubt that fact. If you're an observant person, you know what I'm about to tell you even if it hasn't hit you square between the eyes yet. How many stores in that mall are not a franchise or part of a chain? In many malls, the answer is a big fat zero. In others, not more than a handful. Why the malls are dominated by franchises and chains is a question you should ask yourself. The chains, whether regional or national, are generally well established. They have access to financing and can support a store until it becomes profitable. They are properly capitalized. "But why do the franchises last in the mall?" :::applause::: Great question! I'm glad you asked! Franchises are owned by individuals just like you and me. They had a dream to work for themselves, and decided to purchase a franchise to accomplish that dream. Franchise ownership doesn't guarantee survival, but a much larger percentage of franchises survive as opposed to non-franchise businesses. Your first reaction may be to think that there must be something magical about buying a franchise; some special something that makes them successful while so many others fail. Although a good franchise can offer you many benefits, the true reason for their longevity and success does not lie within the franchise itself. Most storefront franchises, i.e. McDonalds, Subway, Hallmark, etc., require the franchisee to have a certain level of net worth or the potential franchisee will be denied the franchise. McDonalds, for example, requires a net worth of over one million dollars to purchase a franchise. By requiring a certain net worth, the franchise is ensuring that you have the staying power to hold on until the franchise can become profitable. Therefore, the 'magic' doesn't lie within the franchise itself, but is simply properly capitalized. The franchise system weeds out those who don't have the reserves to hang on until the store enters the black.

In the rest of the business world, there is no one requiring a certain level of capital to start a business. It's much easier to have a higher success rate if you keep all of the under capitalized, would-be owners out there from getting into business. As a result, the success rate of franchises is high and the success rate of non-franchise start-ups is very low. So, before you buy into an established franchise because of the high rate of success, take a long hard look at the capital you have available to you. If you have enough capital to get over the bar set by the franchise, you have enough capital to fund your own business based upon your own ideas.

Reason #2. A lack of understanding. No, I'm not talking about com-passion. This is the second largest reason businesses fail, and it is inherently tied to reason number one. Without a doubt…can't change it…you may as well get used to it…make the best of it…all storefronts have seasonal cycles. Let me repeat that more slowly so that ::::::glances back at the title of reason #2:::::: you understand. All storefronts have a
SEASONALCYCLE

I promise to you here and now, with my right hand raised…*if you don't understand the seasonal nature of your business, your business will starve to death from a lack of capital.* So, raise your right hand and repeat after me…come on….raise your hand…I'm not kidding…I'm not writing another word until you raise that hand!!!

::::::tapping foot::::::

OK…that's better. Now, repeat after me….and keep your hand raised.

I swear

::::::you repeat::::::

I will learn and understand

::::::you repeat::::::

the seasonal cycles

::::::you repeat::::::

of my business,

::::::you repeat::::::

and PLAN and ANTICIPATE

::::::you repeat::::::

the effect on my business,

::::::you repeat::::::

and learn and understand

::::::you repeat::::::

how to use and take advantage

::::::you repeat::::::

of those seasonal cycles.

::::::you repeat::::::
You did very well, so you can put your hand down now.

Why is it important to understand the seasonal cycle of your business? Let's take a look at a typical mall store for the answer. If you own a gift shop in a mall, it is well within reason that fully one half of your entire year's worth of sales will take place in November and December. You can also count on January being your slowest month of the year. As a result, if you open your doors for the first time on January 1st expecting your wealth to skyrocket, you've got about a ten month wait. The only expense you have that will track with your sales is the cost of your product. That means ten months of your year the store will either lose money or break even. The term 'Black Friday' was coined by retailers because it is typically the day that puts the retailers in the black for the first time that calendar year. I'm sure most husbands thought the day after Thanksgiving was called 'Black Friday' for very different reasons. But then again, what husband wouldn't give everything he had for the chance to go shopping with his wife on the busiest shopping day of the year? As for me...well...let's just say I've left more than a few marks in the asphalt as my wife dragged me kicking and screaming.

If you're paying attention, you may have asked yourself, "If I lose money or break even ten months out of the year, why not just open a store for the months of November and December?" Excellent question! The answer is because it rarely works. 'Seasonal' stores have a very low return rate, and the reason is that the mall bleeds them dry. 'Seasonal' stores are where the malls really try and get their piece of the seasonal dollar pie. The 'all year' stores have two advantages over the 'seasonal' stores:

1. By being there for the prior ten months, they have advertised themselves to the shopping community for all of those ten months. 'All year' or permanent stores do more seasonal business than do the 'seasonal' stores because the customer knows them and knows that they are there.

2. The permanent stores pay the same rent for November and December as they do the rest of the year. Seasonal stores can pay three to ten times the regular monthly rate to the mall. The malls call it a seasonal rate, but legalized extortion is a much better and more accurate phrase. The typical seasonal store will be lucky to make enough profit to pay the elevated rent charged by the mall. I want to ::::::notices a raised hand in the audience:::::: "Am I doomed to live at the mercy of these seasonal cycles? Is there nothing I can do to stabilize my cash flow?" ::::::standing ovation, lots of clapping:::::: Those are two INCREDIBLE questions! I'm so glad you asked! You have made me ::::::sniff, sniff…so dawg gone proud ::::::wipes a tear::::::

Those nasty seasonal cycles may have their way with your storefront, but you don't have to let them have their way with you and your cash flow. Before we go too far, let's remember that the seasonal cycle of each type of store is different. We have used mall stores in our example because their seasonal nature is so stark. All stores have seasonal cycles, however, but they are often very different.

1. Garden supply stores: Peak-Spring and Fall

2. Building supply stores: Peak-Spring and Summer

3. Indoor flea markets: Peak-Late Fall to Early Spring

4. Swimming pool companies: Peak-Spring and Summer

5. Heating and Air conditioning companies: Peak-Winter and Summer

6. Sporting goods stores: Peak-Spring and Summer

7. Movie theaters: Peak-Winter and Summer

8. Video rental stores: Peak-Fall and Winter

9. Car wash and detail shops: Peak-Spring and Summer

The list can continue for as many types of stores as you can imagine. I didn't mention restaurants because there are so many factors that affect their cycles.

Must you live at the whim of this seasonal monster? Is there nothing you can do to drive these cycles into the depths of the hell from which they rose? ::::::standing on soapbox:::::: Will you suffer forever at their feet?!?!?!?!?!?!? Nay! I say Nay!!! Drive that seasonal devil back to the darkest confines of the earth. ::::::shakes head and regains composure:::::: Sorry, lost myself for a moment. But it is never a bad idea to view seasonal cycles as an entity, because it is an entity. Seasonal cycles exist not because they are a fact in and of themselves. Seasonal cycles are people. They are made up of the buying habits of each and every one of us. A seasonal cycle never bought one thing in a store, never got its' car washed, and never went out to eat a meal. We, as customers, have a tendency to buy seasonally and buy as a member of the herd. If you treat a cycle as a living, breathing thing, you will have a much better understanding of how to take advantage of the cycles. And that, my friends, is the key. Don't try to beat the cycles. Take advantage of the cycles. If you can learn to take advantage of your seasonal cycles, you will be light years ahead of your competition. Most business owners live within the confines set by the cycles. But, if your business lives within those confines, it is confined. Break out and make the cycles work for you.

So…the question remains…how do you make the cycles work for you?

Well…I'm a notta gonna tella you yetta (I suddenly feel like eating some Italian food). You need to read through the next several chapters to understand what you will need to do to make the cycles work for you. ::::::Starts to walk away:::::: What?

Oh…yes…we will be going over all the mechanics of trademarks, logos, etc., but a time and place for everything, and most certainly understanding your business and how to market it comes first. You'll do a much better job designing logos, writing literature, and so on if you have a solid handle on what you are going to do and how you're going to sell it to your customer.

::::::perk:::::: I heard you! And yes, even if you are opening a storefront you need to read the chapters on the other kinds of businesses. So…go do it! ::::::mumbling:::::: *I can't believe they'd skip over those chapters to get to the cycle information; just makes me…* Oh…you're still here ::::::points to next chapter:::::: Go on…you can do it…turn the page and get to reading about service companies.

CHAPTER SIX

▼

SERVICE BUSINESSES

First of all, remember the term 'Service' company has nothing to do with customer service. All companies must have superior customer service if they are to succeed and dominate their competition. A service business, however, is based upon the idea of selling a service rather than a manufactured product. By no means does that mean you cannot sell physical products as well. If a service business is not selling a physical product in addition to or in support of their services, they are missing out on an incredible profit opportunity. Service companies can often get away with a far greater markup on their physical products than can a storefront. The reason being the person performing the service is viewed as the 'expert' in the eyes of the customer. They feel as if they are getting the 'inside' scoop and getting access to products that only a professional can have. It makes them feel as if they are buying something special. As a result they expect to pay a higher price than they would for a similar product off the shelf, so don't disappoint them. There is no service business that exists than cannot find or develop a physical product to sell along with the services they offer

to their customers. I…oh…yes…go ahead…:::::::listening to question::::::
Oh my…and I was so proud earlier of your incredible questions. :::::::shak-
ing head:::::: You shouldn't worry about losing the customer if you sell
product to them. They didn't hire your services to purchase your products
so that they wouldn't need you anymore. They hired your services because
they don't want to do that service themselves. Let's take a look at a cleaning business. You or your employees enter a customer's home or office,
clean each room, and maybe even steam clean the carpets. You tell them of
products you have that they can use for cleaning purposes. When you
make that sale, do you worry that they will never call you again?
:::::::Crossing fingers hoping you get the answer right:::::: The answer is….
"It's according to how you sold it." If you tell the customer, "YOU buy
this and you won't ever need me again," then you lose. The only way you'll
get that customer back is banking on their laziness, lack of time, or incompetence at using the product. But, if you say, "This would be an excellent
product to deal with those problem spots that happen between our visits
to your home or business," then you are looking out for their interests.
The customer will be very pleased that you care about them even when
you're not there. In their mind, you will have cared about them enough to
sell them a product so that they don't have to call you in for a small spot
here or there between appointments. Spot visits are expensive, and by selling product to them, you have saved them money. Packaging your sales
pitch means everything. Package it wrong and you lose a customer, package it right and you have endeared yourself to the customer by supposedly
putting their needs above your own. The trick is that by elevating the
needs of the customer above your own, you elevate your own needs above
theirs…if that makes any sense.

If you'll indulge me for a moment I shall digress. Several years ago, I
was visiting with a client about my products. We reviewed the customer's
needs, and he had needs in four product areas. I was able to supply product for him to test for three of those areas. When we got to the fourth, I
recommended to him a competitor's product, and told him I did not have

a product that would fit that need. I then proceeded to tell him everything he would need to know about my competitor's product so that he would be able to effectively test and evaluate it in his program. His jaw hung open for what seemed like at least a minute. I asked him what was wrong, and he said he'd never heard of a salesman recommending someone else's product before. He even asked me about a product I had that went head to head with the competitor. I told him that, for his sales area, my product was second best, and he should go with the other. I told him that it was my job to see that he had the best product, and if that meant stepping aside on one out of four, so be it. I then reaffirmed that the other three, however, were superior, and he should move them through his testing program quickly to gain the edge over his competition. Over the next several years that customer called me to gain my advise on not only my own product, but I was the one he called about everyone's products. He had learned to trust my advise because he knew I had his best interest at heart.

By having his best interest at heart, and passing up a sale that day on that one potential product line, did I lose….or did I gain? Most salespeople think that getting that sale would have been the most important thing. They operate under the 'live for today' motto of sales. By passing on that sales opportunity I avoided a customer seeing my product fail against a competitor, I gained the other three slots by sacrificing the one, and I became the trusted advisor of that customer. By becoming his advisor, I was able to tell him "You need to do this," and he did it. It meant I got sales and I walked away from sales. But I no longer had to 'sell' him. What I said to him was considered gospel, and I never had to 'pitch' product to him again. By putting his needs above my needs, I placed my own needs at the top of the heap. A customer's needs and your own are not mutually exclusive. If you look out for the needs of your customers, they will look out for yours with a passion. There is nothing more exciting, and absolutely impossible for a competitor to overcome, than a fiercely loyal customer. I have had several competitors call me, sometimes chuckling, sometimes none too pleased, because that customer tells them he'll get back to them once he has Don take a look at their material. And the biggest trick of all...it's not hard to get a customer to become that loyal. Most businesses don't look out for the best interest of the customer. If you do...you will make it...because most of your competition doesn't.

OK, time to recover from having digressed, and get back to the subject at hand...pardon me a moment ::::::glancing back up to check the title of this chapter:::::: Ah...yes...service companies...let's see...where was I? {reading through the previous page or so} yes...uh-huh...oh...that part was good...::::::laughs, remembering a furious competitor or two:::::: and...ah...OK...I'm back.

Service companies, more than all others, must make superior service a part of their daily mantra. The name alone implies customer service, even though that is not the meaning for the term in the application of a service company. One of the reasons is the intimacy inherent in the relationship between a customer and a service company. If you have a cleaning service, you are in the home or office of your customers. If you operate a security service that shreds sensitive documents for companies, you have access to extraordinarily private documents, potentially damaging to that company's position in the marketplace should plans, designs, etc., fall into the hands of their competitors. Any service performed for a customer by a service-oriented company is extremely intimate. This intimacy requires a high degree of trust and customer service. Many service companies even have keys to the homes or businesses that they serve. Compare the two...when a potential customer enters a storefront, the customer is on the property of the store, not their own. The relationship is only as personal as the customer and the store employee or owner allows. The customer rarely feels threatened or violated, because he/she can simply walk out the door of the store and go elsewhere. This gives the customer a feeling of safety because they are in control of the relationship. In this type of relationship, the sales person must lead by allowing the customer to lead. A good sales person will be able to allow the customers to lead themselves to a purchase by gently nudging them down the correct path with the right questions. Always remember…the amount of talking you do will often be inversely proportional to your sales. Know what questions to ask, and let you customer do the talking. It gives the customer a feeling of control, and there is nothing people love to do more than talk about themselves, or tell you what they want and how the last salesperson didn't get it right. Leading by allowing a customer to believe they are leading the conversation is as much art form as skill. Some people can do it naturally, some need to practice to make it flow naturally. If you have a genuine desire to do whatever it takes to make a customer happy, it will often flow naturally once you learn the basic questions to ask. Essentially, you are simply going to ask the customer what they want, and direct the flow of the conversation from that point. As they state what they want, ask questions based upon what they say, and as they answer those, ask more questions. Do this until you and the customer have arrived at the destination together, which is your product. One of the masters at this (and whose tapes I would highly recommend) is Zig Ziglar.

Alas, I digress {may as well get used to it…I do it often…so make sure to read the whole book…no skipping…you just never know when a totally unrelated tidbit is going to pop out at you}.

The issue of intimacy is a serious one, and should never be taken lightly. The trust that is placed in you by your customer is a fragile trust…easily lost. If a person has a bad experience in a restaurant or a store, often the situation can be smoothed over with a kind word, a coupon, a free meal, etc. But if you betray the trust of a service customer, they are often gone forever, with no hope of recovery. I will also promise you that a betrayed service customer will make sure everyone they know will know about their dissatisfaction with your company.

Whether it is a home or a business that has hired your services, you should assume you are being watched. Even though many service companies perform their services when the client is not around, do not assume you are completely alone. Although most people and businesses don't have surveillance within their home or business, assume they do. I'm not saying this to assume that you would do anything potentially dishonest if given the chance. There are many things someone can do to lose a customer that don't involve criminal activity. Let's take a look at a real world example that really did happen, and cost a cleaning company a good contract with a local business. Company A comes alive in the morning when their employees arrive to take on another day. What do you think appears on the security tapes from the night before? A criminal act? Rifling of company documents? Cleaning people being nosy going through desks? No....just a cleaning employee sitting in the chair of the CEO, feet up on the desk, and drool coming out the side of his mouth while he snored to beat the band. After a relaxing two-hour nap, the man got up and resumed his duties. Now, you may think it harsh that the CEO called the owner of the cleaning service in and, after showing him the tape, fired their company. You would think a CEO would understand a lazy employee, simply ask that it not happen again, and make it clear that if it does happen again, the cleaning service would be out of there. Well...there was a bit of a complication...the drooler sitting in the chair of the CEO was the owner of the cleaning service. Think about that for a moment...the owner of the cleaning service, hired by this company, was the one sitting in the chair of the CEO, snoring and drooling. If you think about that long and hard, you will understand why that cleaning service was fired with no second chance. If the owner has no respect for his customers, how will the employees ever have respect for his customers? The owner of the cleaning company himself had violated the trust. There was no one to reprimand, no one to correct, no one the cleaning company owner could point to and tell the customer, "I'll fix that." The owner himself had shown the disrespect to the CEO, leaving only the one course of action.

You will, from time to time, have fires to put out, so you may as well be ready for them. Since most service companies perform their service on the premises of the customer, make sure you and your employees are all properly bonded. You need to do this, first of all because most states require it, but secondly, you will have the occasional bad employee. If you have an employee that steals from a customer, does damage to their property, does something that will result in you being sued by your customer, you will need to be bonded to protect yourself. Bonding will allow you to get insurance that will protect you by compensating the customer for any losses that are a result of the actions of an employee of your company during the course of performing the services for which your company was hired. If you or your customer discover misconduct of some kind performed by one of your employees, you have a very small time frame to set it right, if you are to retain your customer. You will need to know your customer well enough to know what kind of action will satisfy them and allow you to keep their business. You will also have to measure within yourself how far you are willing to go to keep the customer, based upon the misconduct of your employee. If your employee took a soft drink from the refrigerator of the break room when it is supposed to be off limits to your employees, firing would be rather severe. If the customer is demanding the employee be fired for such a minor infraction, you may have to decide between your principles and your customer. An apology would certainly be within reasonable bounds, but, if the employee is unwilling to give an apology, then, of course, termination would be understandable. If the employee apologizes, but continues in the behavior, then, again, termination would be understandable. If the customer is unwilling to accept an apology for such a minor infraction, you will be in an unenviable position, but I guarantee you…sacrificing principles is never a good idea, and will become easier each time.

So…you're taking care of your customers, you're putting out the fires that crop up…what can you do that will set you apart from every other company that does what you do? Boy…that's a tough one isn't it? Or…is it? What makes you feel special? What puts a smile on your face when it's you being take care of by a company? First, of course, is good service. Second, is the indescribable something that will make each and every employee of a business think of your name and no one else's. Let me take a minute here to ask you a question…I promise it won't take away from your book time…really, I swear. What hotels do you enjoy most, and what is it they do that makes them better than other hotels in which you may stay from time to time? If you go down the list, you might be surprised at the tiny little thing or things that make you prefer one hotel over another. I can tell you the most common thing that brings a smile to the face of a traveler is that little mint they find on their pillow. A small five or ten cent item is what most travelers say they miss when it's not there. Something they can do for themselves by buying a bag of mints for a couple of dollars and bringing it with them…and yet it's what they look forward to when they stay at a hotel. What little thing is it you can do to keep your name in the forefront of your customer's mind. What little thing can you do to tighten your relationship with the customer, making it harder for your competition to take them away from you? Sticking with our cleaning service example, why not leave mints the same way a hotel service would? If that would be too cumbersome, such as in a large office, could you leave a box of donuts in the break room? You could leave fruit, pastries, anything that would ingratiate yourself to your customer or the employees of the customer. If you choose to leave things in the break room for the employees of your customer, stand a thank you note next to the box, thanking them for their business. No sense in leaving a gift and not getting the credit for it…when it is your intent to make your gratitude for their business evident.

Now that we've covered how to take care of…and kiss up to…your customers, how do you find them. How do you market your product when your product is your ability to perform a service. As with any business, you need to develop a profile of your potential customer base. For this example, let's use a pest control service, even though the process is the same for any service business. Pest control services seek out both business and residential customers. How do you go about getting your name in front of those customers? Do you advertise in the newspaper? Direct mail? Radio? Television? You can do those, but if those are all you do, you will just be throwing yourself into a large pot with all of your competition, and hoping you get picked. Once you get picked you can WOW them with your superior service....but you have to get picked first.

Your approach to the problem of getting noticed will be quite different for business than it will for residential. Although the methods for finding customers vary by type of customer, the key to finding them is the same...networking. My head nearly explodes saying the word. It's become a word that is exceedingly overused and corrupted by elite minded people who view networking as a schmooze event. We all network, nearly each and every day, and you probably don't even know you're doing the network thing. If I asked you where to find a good auto repair place, you would most likely have an answer. No matter what I mention, you would most likely, have a particular place or person you would recommend to me. You have a network of people and businesses in place that can do the things you need done from time to time. With your business you are now going to do it conscientiously and with determination. So...let's get to networking!

Ahhhhhhhhh ::::::breathes deeply:::::: Doesn't the office of your new pest control business smell wonderful? ::::::looking around:::::: I love what you've done with the place, and the giant bug on the roof certainly was...ummmm...well...it's so...unique...yeah, that's it...unique... ::::::whew::::::

So...we're standing in your bright, shiny, new office, and you don't have one single customer. Where do you go? We just talked about networking, so let's try and see what that does for us. First, we'll start with residential customers. If you need to get your feet wet, best to do it with a small account than land a big one and lose it because you weren't ready. How do you go about getting those residential customers? If advertising is in your start-up budget, then get to it. Check into newspaper, direct mail, television, radio, and local magazines. Get your name out so people see and hear it everywhere. Remember to target your audience in your advertising. If you're on radio, advertise on home repair shows, gardening shows, even shows about investing. I know it may, at first glance, seem like a stretch, but a radio ad on an investment show can work if the ad is tailored for that show. Think about it for a moment, "Your home is the biggest investment you make, protect it by calling us today." I think you catch the meaning here. Tailor your ads to the show on which they will run. In newspapers, advertise in the real estate section, the gardening section, home repair section, sports section, and the investment section. Just make sure to tailor the ad for the section of the paper in which it will run.

You are now advertising…but we haven't done the big network thing yet. To gain residential clients networking will be imperative. It can get your foot in the door before any of your competition even knows a door is there. There are as many opportunities to network as you have the imagination to dream about. Two big ones are real estate agents and homebuilders. Visit with every real estate company, agent, and homebuilder you can find in your area. Try to build a relationship with them. Your goal is to get them on your side and have them out there selling your service for you…at the very least, giving you the names of the people to whom they have sold or built homes. Develop a referral package and propose it to them. Agents and builders are always looking for additional sources of income, so offer them referral fees for all the business they send your way.

If there is a welcoming service in your town, such as Welcome Wagon, make sure your service is tied into them. Include in their welcome kit a coupon for services, a refrigerator magnet, etc. day cares, schools, little leagues, or any organization that raises money for projects is a source of new customers. Offer to help them do a fund-raiser by offering them a set dollar amount for each service of yours that they sell. Do tie-ins with non-competing businesses. Find other businesses in your area that are in non-competing fields, and do advertising swaps. For example, on your sales form you may have ads for three other companies: ABC Auto Repair, DEF Hardware, and GHI Bait and Tackle. On all of their sales slips would be an ad for your pest business. The four of you don't compete against one another, but each of your businesses is now exposed to the customer base of all four of your businesses. It doesn't have to stop at sales slips either. You could put up signs for each other's businesses in your stores, run joint ads in the newspaper, and anything else you can imagine. The point is that you have each exposed your company to a wider base for no additional advertising costs. Be careful when arranging cooperative advertising, however. Some matches are not made in heaven. The obvious match to avoid is promoting business of a direct competitor. Another match to avoid is exchanging advertising with a company when the match would be repulsive to the customer. For example, our brand new pest company would never want to exchange advertising with a restaurant...'After you eat at Joe's, don't forget to take care of that cockroach problem,' just wouldn't be very appealing ad copy to someone sitting down to a meal. Likewise, I would be afraid to eat at a restaurant that has a sign advertising your pest company in the window. So...make sure the matches fit...or you could end up driving customers away instead of bringing them to your door.

OK...we're working like gangbusters to build that residential network of contacts, and you're ready to tackle the business world. Dreams of huge contracts are floating through your head, and you're ready for the big time. Well, compadre...I don't want to be the one to burst your bubble, but don't ever forget....most businesses are small business. The big corporate giants are few, and the contracts hard to get. Getting one of the big boy contracts will take a lot of time, and most likely a lot of presentations, as you work your way through the corporate structure one meeting at a time. Don't let that stop you though. Even if it takes a year or more to land one of those big accounts, it will most certainly be worth the time and effort once you have accomplished the task. But...be ready! You will need to service the account to death to keep it...because you can be guaranteed someone else is going through the long process of meetings to try and take that account away from you. Make sure your big time customer is so pleased with you they would never dream of leaving. To accomplish this, you need to make sure your name stays in front of the faces that hired you. If they forget your name, then it will simply be a matter of price when the next person works their way through the corporate structure. It can be difficult to make a relationship personal in a large corporate environment, but you must do it to ensure your ability to keep that client. Send them monthly updates on the services you have performed. Send them reminders of the next month's services you will be performing. Check with them as to what events will be occurring at their business the next month, so as to establish the best time for you to perform your duties. Send them cards thanking them for their business. Learn their birthdays, the birthdays of their family, and send cards to them. Learn their interests. Oh my…I feel a digression coming on…

I remember a customer who had purchased small quantities of testing material from me several times, but I could never seem to break through. In addition to selling product to him, I had wanted to source some of the goods they manufactured, and represent that material on the wholesale market. He was a very busy man that spent little time in his office, so I had always seen him in testing labs or the production facilities. One day he had more time than normal, and we went to his office. On every shelf, bookcase, desk, and filing cabinet were metal scale models of old farm tractors. I never said a word about it…but filed it away in my head. I tracked down one of the best books I could find about old tractors, with color pictures of the restored models included within the pages. The next time I called on him, I presented him with the book. For the little extra, I had gotten in touch with the publisher and arranged to get the copy signed by the author with the inscription being written to my customer. He was amazed I had gone to so much trouble, and was greatly touched by the gift. That year his company began sending material my way, allowing me to act as their wholesale agent. He also began using more of my products in his own sales effort. I don't tell the story to try and get you to go out and bribe your customers to do business with you. If you present the gift as a bribe, it will never fly. You are simply trying to establish a personal connection with the client…by finding out more about your customer. The more you know about your customer, the more they will view their relationship with you as one of friendship, as opposed to simply being a

vendor. ::::::scanning back to see where I was before digressing::::::
Oh…yes…OK…back to it then, shall we?…::::::clearing throat::::::

Send anniversary cards, Christmas cards, updates on any law changes in
OSHA, pest control, etc., that may have an effect upon their business. Just
do what it takes to make the relationship personal. It's a lot easier for me
to fire the ABC Pest Company than it is to fire my pal Bob, whom I go
golfing with once in a while.

We went over how to keep the business client once you get him, but
where will you find him? Join your local chamber of commerce. It is a
great source of information about the businesses in your community. You
will receive a members directory that will provide you with all the contact
names you will need to start looking for your customers. You can also join
professional organizations, Kiwanis, Rotary, business clubs, lead clubs,
and any other organization that will be attended by other business repre-
sentatives Lead clubs can be especially productive. One of the largest is
Business Network International. They are national, so check your local
newspaper in the business meeting calendar. Lead clubs get together on a
regular basis, and are typically comprised of only one company per type of
business. This way they don't have competing members sitting around the
same breakfast table. The members eat a meal, discuss marketing ideas,
and give each other leads based upon recent sales in their own business.
You may have a pest control customer that you know is new to the area,
maybe you relay the information regarding the new residents along to the
dentist of the group.

So…let's go back and re-cap the service business 'must do' list:

1. Advertise

2. Network

3. Know your customer on a personal level

4. Service the stuffing out of your customers

5. Keep your name in front of them at all times—magnets, thank you notes, gifts, reminders, newsletters, and anything else you can do to make them remember you.

Take a deep breath…::::::::in…out::::::OK…let's get ready for the next chapter…shall we? I'll take a quick peek ahead…ahhhhhhhhh….mail order companies. Now remember….all business have components you can use in your business, so I'll say it again…don't skip a chapter just because you think it has nothing to do with your business. As much as I digress, you never know when you'll read something that you'll want to mark up with that big yellow highlighter…. Soooo…. onward and upward…and Chapter 7…

CHAPTER SEVEN

▼

MAIL ORDER COMPANIES

{Empty room...you hear footsteps coming around the corner} Wooooooo, what a workout! ::::::stretching legs, bending sideways:::::: Sorry I'm late. I thought it would take you a bit longer to turn the page, so I went to do a bit of lifting. Pardon me a moment while I towel off this sweat. I'd hate to splatter you during a particularly exciting part of this chapter. {Towel, towel, dry, dry} Ahhhhh....much better! Nothing keeps the muscles firm and in shape like lifting all those nasty catalogs I get in the mail. I just tie a bunch of them together and use them as weights. {Glances up at the title of this chapter}...Ooopps, sorry. Hey! At least I have a use for them. Most people throw away the catalogs they receive in the mail without even looking at them. At least I'm getting some exercise from them. I wonder why companies spend all that money on publishing and postage, when they could save themselves a lot of money by throwing their catalogs in the trash themselves? Hmmmmmmmm...sounds like something we should talk about a little later. For now, though, let's start at the beginning.

I was born on a small farm in southern Indiana back in 19…uh…not that far back? OK, I'll just start at the point where you decide to do a mail order business. Sound good?…Good!

Unless you are a national retail chain with millions to spend on catalogs, you will have to maintain a focus in your mail order materials. You may ask what I mean by focus. Think of the catalogs you receive through the mail. I would be willing to wager that they are of three essential types:

1. Major national retailers-JC Penney, Service Merchandise, etc.

2. Inexpensive eclectic merchandisers-An example of this type of mail order company would be Fingerhut.

3. Specialty merchandisers-This covers the vast majority of mail order catalogs sent to homes and businesses each year. They can range from goods for a specific industry to the latest and hottest must have science fiction merchandise to food products.

Whatever product line you decide to sell through the mail, you must remember the three main categories of people to whom you are sending your catalog.

1. Repeat customers-They have purchased from you more than once, and as long as they continue to be pleased with the product and your service, they will hopefully continue to do so. Assuming this continued satisfaction, they will keep your catalog as reference material for possible future purchases.

2. First time buyers-They have made one purchase from your company, and, as such, you can't be sure whether they can be considered a future repeat customer. Do everything you can to make sure they are pleased with the product and the service they receive from your company.

3. Non-purchasers-These people have received multiple catalogs from you and have never purchased anything. They could have no interest

in your products. They could be catalog window shoppers, look-ing....but never buying. They could also be the people you're losing because your catalog didn't grab them and hold their attention.

Let's speak on this last category of buyers for a moment. When you send a catalog to someone for the first time, that person is an unknown. We all receive an inordinate amount of what we all call junk mail each and every year. Through the constant barrage of unsolicited mail, we have developed certain patterns to deal with junk mail. That pattern is typically to not even read it in the first place....just send it on it's way straight to the trash. From the time that new potential customer picks up your catalog from the rest of their mail, you can assume it is on its' way to the waste-basket. For many, it's one sweeping arc of the arm...pick up catalog.....moving upward in an arc towards the eyes so that they can see it...then the arc begins its' descent toward the wastebasket. Your catalog has that small amount of time to reach up, grab the reader, and yell in his face, "Hey! At least look inside before you throw me away!" The only thing that can halt that arc and keep your catalog from joining the rest of the 'junk' mail in the circular file is the catalog cover. It must grab the reader quickly, and hold him long enough to tempt him to take a look inside. But.....how do you get a catalog cover to reach out and grab the reader...and make them look inside? Well.....get the gear together, because we're going fishing, and, just like fishing, you need a hook. The hook is going to be that 'something' that gets the reader to stop before throwing away your catalog. Your hook has got to get the customer to bite on it, and it has to sink in and not let go. You want to make sure that customer isn't going to get another good night's sleep until they get some product from you. You want to make them want your product so badly that you hear them ask, "How much for rush delivery?" You want to create a catalog and a cover that, when you look at it, will make you feel almost sorry for the customer, because they have no hope of resisting your masterpiece.

You have two possible places for your hook, depending on whether or not you use an envelope in which to mail your catalog. You will have to balance the cost of an envelope against the benefits, and decide for yourself whether or not to use them. An envelope will add to your printing, labor, and possibly your postage costs. The benefits can be significant, however. An envelope helps to keep the appearance of your catalog clean and neat. Unprotected catalogs can get beaten quite severely through the US Postal Service. The post office is not known for it's gentle treatment of material, so your catalogs may arrive at their destination in less than impressing fashion. An envelope will also be a great double-edged sword. It will give you the opportunity to set a double hook by grabbing the attention of the reader with the envelope, and grabbing onto it even harder with the catalog cover. The flip side of that is you can create an incredible catalog cover, but a weak envelope. If the envelope is weak, the great catalog cover will never be seen, because the envelope won't be opened before it goes into the trash. A strong envelope can also help to offset an average catalog cover by piquing enough interest to get the reader past the average cover. If you decide to use an envelope, grab the reader's attention without using sleazy gimmicks. How many times have you opened mail because it looked like it came for the United States government? Or because the envelope said you won a prize? Or the envelope said it had urgent tax information? The list is endless, but when you opened the mail…were you glad they had used those means to trick you into opening the mail they had sent? Most people get upset when they are tricked into opening a piece of mail that they would normally throw into the trash. You want the customer to be happy that they have looked through your catalog…so don't use tricks. Get the reader to walk through the door voluntarily, and you will be more likely to gain a customer.

As you prepare your catalogs and envelopes to be mailed, always know the differences between the people receiving your catalogs. Break them down according to the categories we covered earlier. If you use an envelope, you have a very easy way to tailor the mail to each type of potential customer. For your repeat customers, the hook isn't to get them to open the catalog, it should be to get them to make steady purchases each and every time they see your catalog in the mail. Your hook could be discounts for repeat buyers, sending a short-lived coupon with every catalog, advertising a cumulative point system, buyer referral offers, and/or anything else you can dream up to keep them buying. You have a few days to get an order from them before they forget about your catalog sitting in the magazine rack, so make them want to act quickly. The tricky question is what to do with a repeat customer when they have apparently stopped ordering product. Are they not ordering product because you have nothing they wish to purchase? Did your catalog not entice them? Was the hook ineffective? Did their financial situation become such that they can no longer afford to purchase your products? The customer that once purchased from you, but no longer does, can be the one that costs you a fortune in printing and postage fees. Every time a catalog goes out your door, you should expect an order. When that order does not arrive, you should have a plan in place to deal with the offending party (my little term for people who don't order). You must have so much confidence in your product that you are amazed any time someone doesn't place an immediate order. Your response to non-orders from repeat customers should be included with your next mailed catalog. When it comes to new prospects, they should be on your 'one and gone' list. With the millions of people who are your potential customers, your time and money is best served seeking a new prospect…not continuing to try and pry money out of prospects that have never ordered product. To drop people from your mailing list, you need to have confidence in your hook. Doubt will cost you a lot of money as you keep cranking catalogs out to window shoppers who will never place an order. Put firm plans in place on how you respond to each type of offender. With a set plan in place, you will avoid the pitfall of doubt. For an entrepreneur, doubt is a cancer that will eat you for breakfast. You'll spend your entire day wondering, "Is my hook good? Should I send one more catalog? Maybe they'd order this time. What if I did this? What if I did that?" Be confident of your product. Be confident in your hooks. Be confident in how you handle people who don't order. Then stick to your plans. When you need to drop people…drop them! When you need to offer incentives…offer them! There are many ways to encourage continued buying. Some we have already gone over. You will come up with some tailored to your products and your personal style. One thing you can do which I personally have never seen in mail order is something I alluded to a page or so back. You may lose customers now and then through no fault of your own. They may still love your product, but through some financial crisis, must cut back on their spending. Translation: No catalog orders. Yet, even these people will buy Christmas gifts, necessities, clothing, etc. How can you get them to buy through you instead of the local stores to which they have access? For years and years, banks have been offering Christmas clubs to help people save for their gift buying. Many people have enjoyed them because it allows them to spread the cost of their buying over the course of a year, as opposed to spending in a lump sum. This concept has never been adopted for business…and it is an untapped marketing boon. Let us suppose you have a catalog that sells gift items. You could offer a Christmas or gift buying savings or payment plan to your customers. The customer sends a pre-arranged dollar amount each month. This dollar amount can be set to automatically bill to their credit card, or you can send them a bill through the mail each month. Through your program, you could offer to add 10% to their account at the end of the year. The customer gets ten percent on his money, and can spread the cost of gifts over twelve months. You have helped to keep a customer that you would have otherwise lost. Now…on your part…you have to make sure to put that money in the bank, and…whatever you do….don't touch it! Don't pull out any of that money until the customer has placed an order for product. You may then pull that amount only. Leave any of the customer's unused funds in the account. By doing it this way, the money will draw interest, and cut the ten percent you are paying the customer down to five percent or so.

What it all boils down to is being creative. There are a tremendous number of mail order businesses in the United States. You must figure out a way to separate yourself from the crowd. When your prospect opens the mailbox, the clock starts ticking. Your catalog has to sell itself in a matter of a few seconds…or it's in the trash. You must also be ready and willing to drop people…and…be ready to do whatever it takes to keep the others buying. Let your imagination run wild, and make it fun for you…and fun for the customer.

Chapter Eight

▼

Internet Companies

OK…Quiz time!!!! Grab your pencils, eyes forward, and see if you can tell me who made the following statement.

Hey! You…in the back…no cheating!

No…not that statement…this one…

"…the Internet is like a tidal wave. Those who don't learn to swim in it's wake will be drowned by it…"

::::::waiting::::::

::::::humming::::::

No peeking ahead now…what? ::::::ding, ding, ding:::::: Someone got it right! Yes, it was Bill Gates. I feel it would be safe to say that Bill Gates has a success or two in building a business and anticipating market changes. The Internet is becoming a force in the world that has never seen a rival. Nearly one million new sites go up each day, and the rate of growth is increasing at a dizzying pace. Businesses that would take years to reach a million dollars in sales in the real world do so on the Internet in some-times less than a year. Is the Internet a gold mine? Does it represent instant success? If you put up a website, will the money start rolling in by the truckloads? Don't count on it. As with any other business, you need to know what you are doing. To read articles in money maker magazines and the like, it would appear that just having a website will get the money train to come chugging to your door each morning. Promises of instant wealth on the Internet "...without even owning a computer..." are common-place, but these people are today's snake oil salesmen. If you create a new industry, there will be people that figure out how to cheat other people within that industry in short order. You hear them in radio commercials advertising big profits in futures markets, work part-time from home and get rich, buy real estate with nothing down and sell for big profits, and the list goes on and on ad infinitum. In the 1970's, it was buying your own oil well, and who knows how many times the Brooklyn Bridge has been sold over the years.

Now don't, for a moment, think I'm saying stay away from the Internet. Quite the contrary. I am confident that every business had better be on the Internet, and had better get there quickly. Internet business is more than doubling each year, and it is anticipated that it can sustain this growth for years to come. The caution I stated in the preceding paragraph is the same caution you should use in starting any business. Educate your-self and become as informed as you can be. Does it mean you need to learn how to write HTML code? Heaven help me if it does. The programs that say they are designed so that even an idiot can write a webpage stump me. Knowing how to write programs is not necessary to use a computer. I classify myself as a good user, but get me anywhere near code and you may as well speak Chinese to me, because I don't understand either one.

The thing that is important to know about the Internet is how to use it to benefit your business. If the products you sell can be sold over the Internet, then the possibilities are obvious. If you have a service that is very geographic, then maybe your website will be more informational in nature. Whatever your business, the Internet can help your business grow. But, as with anything, it can only help when it is used properly and effectively. To figure out how to do that, you need to know who is on the Internet. The demographics for the Internet are constantly changing as thousands of people jump into the waters for the first time. The salary average of an Internet user is above $60,000. The typical user is a homeowner, owns 2 cars, and has made purchases online. These are prime demographics, and you need to learn how to exploit the opportunities the Internet gives you to reach these people.

So how do you go about it? How do you find these people? Good questions! But the better question is…how are these people going to find you? A few years ago it would have been easy. There were very few businesses on the Internet, so searching for them was not difficult. But today, it can be like trying to find the proverbial needle in a haystack. Run a search for a particular product or service today, and you may get 10,000 or more websites referring to that product. The typical web surfer may scan the search engine for the first 20 to 100, but will rarely go any deeper into the search. I can guarantee you that if your site came up with a high number, it will never be seen. Unfortunately a lot of these sites will be redundant, due to a process I refer to as 'chumming the waters.' Much as you toss the meat and blood over the side of the boat to attract the shark, these people get multiple addresses all leading to their page. The result is that when someone runs a search for their product, up comes 5, 10, 15, 20, or more links all leading to their website. Certainly searching would be much less cumbersome for consumers if these unethical practices were not allowed by the search engines. And, before you get the idea of chumming, think about how irritated you would be if you were searching sites, and kept going to the same site over and over, even though you were under the impression you were linking to a different site. I personally will not do business with a company that chums the waters. By using this practice, they show no regard for their potential customer. Searching can be cumbersome, and sites that chum the water simply exacerbate the problem for the consumer.

After you make the decision to have a website, the task is to write the thing. Unless you're a whiz at writing and designing websites, leave it to a professional. You will be money ahead having a professional design your site…rather than placing a site that looks as if it were built by an amateur in front of the eyes of your customer. This website will have the same impact on your customer as your literature, the entrance to your store, and the appearance of your equipment. That first page of your website will tell them whether or not your site is worth their time, so make it a grabber!

As you sit down with your site designer for the first time, you will need to know the approach you want to take with the site. We are going to take a look at the two primary types of sites separately. Whether it is a commercial site or an informative site, you will be mingling a bit of both, so pay attention to both sections.

Commercial sites.

A commercial site is a virtual store. Just imagine in your mind all of the components to a real world store, and you will be able to easily design your virtual store. One of the striking differences between the two, however, is the size of the store. In the real world, a store that only sold one product would never stay in business. Wouldn't shopping be just terribly exciting if, when you walked into each store, you saw one product sitting on the shelf? You'd never go back, unless they were the only store that sold that one product, and you happened to have a need for that product. On the Internet, however, it is possible to have a 'one product' store and be successful. The opposite is also true. A new entrepreneur starting out goes out into the real world to open a retail store, and quickly gets hit in the face with the reality of how expensive it is to lease square footage. Then the calculator in your head starts spinning the numbers to see just how much profit must be made daily to just pay for the lease. The more products and product lines you carry, the more square footage you need, the higher your rent, the more profit you must make to sustain the business. Alas, tis not the way of things in the virtual world grasshopper. In the virtual world, the size of your store is only limited by how many megs of memory your are renting on a server. If you have 20, 50, or 100 megs of storage, you can have one BIG virtual store. No square footage to lease, no employees to stand at the cash register or re-stock the shelves. No manager to hire to be at the store when you aren't there. And the big Kahuna…the big enchilada…the nasty little bugger that drives so many businesses under because they wallow in it…inventory. With a virtual store, you don't have to have one piece of inventory anywhere near you. No capital tied up in sitting product. No interest being paid on money you had to borrow to buy the product to see in your store. That is the huge advantage with virtual stores, nearly non-existent overhead. In the virtual world, you can appear to be as big as Wal-Mart or any other business in any other industry. One of the biggest online success stories has been Amazon.com, an online bookstore. They have over two million titles for sale…more than any real world bookstore could ever stuff into a physical store. Yet the founder of Amazon.com started this mega bookstore in his garage. Now…unless his garage is bigger than your garage or mine…how could he possibly fit an inventory of over two million books in his garage? The answer is the beautiful thing about Internet stores. Drop shipping. Get to know those two words because they are beauties. You will find that most wholesale suppliers will be thrilled to do drop shipments for you. Oh…sorry…some of you out there may not know what drop shipments are…no problem. Drop shipping works as follows:

1. Your customer places an order through your website and pays for the product and shipping charges via a credit card.

2. You call your supplier for that product(s) and tell them the product to ship and the address to which it is to be shipped.

3. The supplier ships out the product with your name and paperwork on it…and in the package.

4. The supplier bills you for the product and the shipping charges.

5. You pay the supplier for the product and shipping charges.

You may notice that during the entire process, you never saw or took possession of the product. It is entirely feasible, and is the norm in the virtual world, to operate a store selling thousands of products, throughout the entire world, from one computer, sitting at one desk, in one room of someone's home. Small or large has none of the meaning in the virtual world that they do in the physical world. But don't operate under the impression that all is peaches and cream. There will be a price you pay for being able to compete with companies much larger than you are by being on the Internet. That price is speed. When customers buy products through the mail, they expect the standard six to eight weeks. Everyone understands that mail is slow, and they don't expect things to happen quickly. When a customer has a complaint with a business in the physical world, they understand it may take time to resolve their complaint, given a certain hierarchy within the business. In a virtual store, however, none of this is acceptable to a customer. By doing business online, you must learn to do things fast. At most, you have twenty-four hours to respond to a customer before they take their business elsewhere. I highly recommend having an auto-response system. When a customer sends mail to you, the auto responder will send a message back to them immediately confirming that their message has been received. Auto responders can also be set to send a message confirming the order the customer just placed. The auto responder simply tells the customer that their message or order was received. It does not take the place of an e-mail or phone call from you. Make sure you follow-up on your e-mail and orders quickly.

Responses to complaints should always be personalized. Take the time to read the complaints and learn from them. Complaints can be invaluable learning opportunities. They can also be an opportunity to keep a customer by making them feel that you are really listening and care about their satisfaction. Use complaints to your benefit, and don't take them personally. I also recommend you send an e-mail to your customer the day their product is shipped. Again, the shipping of product should happen within twenty-four hours of the time the order was placed. When you send the e-mail to the customer, tell them how it was shipped (UPS, USPS, FedEx, etc.). Tell them how many packages they should expect, and thank them for their business. It should appear to be personalized, even if it is not. Also, include the amount of their total bill. When they order, all they know is the cost of the product, including shipping of their purchase. Often they will not know how much the shipping charges will cost when they place their order. This will allow them to know exactly how much was charged to their credit or debit card.

Now just because you have your own, bright, and shiny new virtual store don't go and get all snobbish. Auction sites are a hot thing on the internet today. Most aren't worth the time it takes to list the items you wish to place for auction, but a few can be a wonderful place not only to sell more product, but to drive people to your virtual store. Ebay is a perfect example of what is right about on-line auctions. By placing some of your product up for auction you can sell more product. You also have the opportunity to advertise your virtual store with every item you sell. In the description portion, you simply let the potential bidder know of your web-site address and that you have wonderful items that they simply must come and see for themselves. Just remember, the internet is a very visual medium, make sure you have the ability to put pictures in your auction so that people can see what it is they are bidding to win. Pictures will allow you to get a higher price for your goods, and increase the chances of being bid upon.

Knowing how to treat the customer is important, but how do you go about finding customers to purchase products from your virtual store? When you open a store in a real world mall you have an idea of the traffic generated through the halls of that mall. Your store, by being in the mall, will be seen by everyone passing through the mall's corridors. If your store is sufficiently enticing, they will come in to shop. This isn't the way of things with a virtual store. No one will know you are there unless you shout it to the world. Mall stores have the luxury of passive advertising if they choose to not advertise. Simply by being there they will get a certain amount of traffic. If you don't advertise and solicit customers, your virtual store will have little or no traffic whatsoever. The only way you can hope to generate any passive traffic to your site is to have your store in a prime Internet mall or community. I personally recommend Geocities.com very highly. They have nearly 2 million websites in their community, and can offer excellent assistance in the promotion of your site. Do you advertise on the Internet? Do you advertise in the physical world? The answer is YES…to both. Just because your store is on the Internet does not mean you get out of advertising in the physical world. Au contrar mon ami (sure hope that's right, and my 1 year of French in High School wasn't for nothing), it becomes even more imperative.

Let's take a look at ways of advertising your site. Now remember, advertising includes advertising your site within your site. If that sounds a little confusing, hold on, and we'll tackle it in a moment. The first thing to do is make sure you get your site tied into all of the search engines available. Unless you're an expert, have your site designer do it for you. There are over 60 search engines at the time of this writing, and new ones coming all the time. Most designers will hook your site to all of them for about one hundred dollars. For the time it would take you to do it, I promise you it's worth the money. You'll have no control as to where you site will appear amongst all the sites pulled up in a search, so don't worry or fret over your placing.

Advertising on the Internet can be a lot of fun. It can also be as time consuming as you will allow it to be. Make sure to budget your time effectively so that you don't ignore other avenues of promotion, or neglect your business itself. There are as many ways of promoting your site as you have the imagination to invent on the Internet. We're going to cover the main three that will be the backbone of your advertising in the virtual world.

1. Newsgroups and Bulletin Boards—For each type of product you sell, you should begin running searches for those products on the Internet. Also, you will want to search for activities related to those products.

Example: One of your product lines is fishing gear.

Search: You would go through and search for each of your products—fishing poles, bait, lures, life jackets, etc.

You would also search for activities that may have to do with your products—fishing, camping, hiking, boating, bass, trout, lakes, recreation, etc.

You could contact any lodges, resorts, wilderness campgrounds, hotels, etc., that cater to fishermen, and see if they would be interested in swapping advertising. They could place flyers about your website in the rooms, cabins, or with the camping maps. In return, you could run banner ads for them on your website. Just like we talked about in chapter five, you should always be looking for opportunities to swap advertising with complimentary businesses. As you go through these searches, you will run across sites that have bulletin boards or newsgroups. Bulletin boards and newsgroups are places where the readers in that site can post messages to other readers. When you find one, make sure to add that location to your favorite places file, so that you can find it again without having to run a search. After locating a bulletin board or newsgroup, post a message briefly describing your business. Offer them some sort of discount if they mention the bulletin board when they place their order. The discount will give them an incentive to visit your site, and it will give you a way of tracking which bulletin board is the most effective for you.

2. Banner Exchanges—if you've been online, you've seen banner ads whether you know it or not. They are the banners that can be anywhere on the page...that advertise another site. When you click on them, you are taken to another location on the web. There are several banner exchange companies, and they are easy to find. Typically, any company that has other banners on their site will also carry a banner for the link exchange site being used. When you get to the link exchange site, you will be able to choose from many links or types of links with which you wish to exchange. I am not aware

of any blind banner exchange sites, but make sure you know what types of businesses will be exchanging banners with you. The last thing you want is to have a family-oriented site and find out that you are exchanging banners with sexually-oriented sites. Make sure that the banner exchange site will provide a list of sites that will be placing your banner on their site. When you get the list, visit each of the sites to reassure yourself that it is a good site for promoting your business. Whether or not you run banners on your site from businesses that compete with you will be your decision. If you have a site that is phenomenal, it can actually be a benefit. The customer will link to the other site and be reassured that when he does business with you, he is at the best site available. If you are considering placing a competitor's banner in your site, go to their site and check them over before you make your decision. Checking out the competition is something that you should always be doing. You never know when you may get an inspiration for a change in your site, and, quite often, seeing someone else's way of building a site will provide just that.

3. Bulk e-mail programs. These go beyond description in how valuable they will be to your virtual store. Now, before we go too far, there is one last word you must learn. It is the online equivalent of those lecherous creatures that call you at home in the evening to try and sell something to you just as you are trying to chew your dinner. These vile, horrible online creatures are known as spammers. Spam is online junk mail. Spammers are the people that keep hitting you over and over for the same thing time and again. The last thing you want to do is to be tagged as a spammer.

::::::steps back to put forth a couple of definitions::::::
ISP—Internet Service Provider—these are companies that give you access to the Internet, i.e. Netscape, locals.

Front-ends—AOL (America Online), CompuServe, Prodigy. These companies have many services on the 'front-end' and also provide access to the Internet.

::::::steps back to where we left off::::::

All front-end companies have procedures in place to deal with spammers. If the front-end company receives enough complaints about you, they will block your mail from going to any of their customers. Some ISP's have procedures in place to block mail, but most do not. You can avoid being labeled a spammer simply by not harassing people that don't respond to your mail. There are millions of people online all over the world. Don't lose your access to them because you wouldn't leave a few of them alone.

Design a solicitation for each of your product lines. When you run your bulk e-mail program, you will type in key words for which it would search across the Internet. Using our fishing example, you would type in all the words we listed for our search…plus any others of which you can think. You would then start the bulk e-mail program on it's task of finding e-mail addresses throughout the Internet of people that have shown interest in those topics. You would typically let it run overnight, as it may take a few hours. The program is, after all, searching through millions of websites to find the information. When it is done, it will have a list of addresses to which you can send your e-mail. Once you send it, make sure you label the address file as being done. You don't want to use it again, unless you wish to run the risk of the spam label. As with any other solicitation, make sure to include a discount or online coupon if they respond within so many days. Make sure the coupon is only good if they respond via e-mail. You want to get a response so that you know who is interested in your products. These people that have shown interest can be added to your regular mailing list, keeping them updated on changes or specials running on your site. Keep your regular mailing list separate from your bulk solicitation mailing lists. Each product line you carry should be solicited separately. Run your bulk e-mail program for each product line using keywords for each product line. Imagine if your site sells a line of cigar products, and also a line of soap products. Someone interested in lilac soaps shaped like seashells may not be terribly interested as to whether or not your Ashton cigar comes in corona or churchill size. You will have a bulk e-mail list for each product line. Write a solicitation for each product line and, for heaven's sake, send the right one with the right e-mail list. Label the lists clearly so that you do it correctly. Make sure to incorporate the date into the filename of the bulk e-mail lists. This will allow you to know when they were retrieved. This will be helpful when you run the same search again in a month or so. You will be able to run a comparison between the two fishing products e-mail lists, and delete the addresses from the new list that were also present on the old list.

There is one bit of business of which you need to be aware. To effectively run a bulk e-mail program, you should run it through an ISP. Front-ends tend to be slow because of the density of traffic over their lines. The customers of an ISP are on the Internet. The customers of a front-end may be on the Internet or they may be within the services offered by the front-end company. Wherever they are, front-ends tend to be very slow in relation to the tasks the bulk e-mailer must perform. In addition, most front-end companies don't like you to run a bulk e-mailer over their lines. They are dense enough with traffic without you adding onto that with the significant traffic generated by a bulk e-mail program. There are plenty of ISP's that can deal with the traffic you will generate. Call them and tell them what you will be doing. The last thing you want is to be hooked to an ISP that bogs down because of the traffic you send through its lines. As with anything, shop around, and find the best ISP, for the money, that can handle the traffic.

One little tidbit I would recommend to you as you design your site. On your website, you will offer methods by which the customer can reach you…phone, fax, physical address, and Internet address. In regard to your Internet address, I would suggest you not place your ISP address or the address provided by your web host. There are many sites, such as your

Hotmail.com, that offer free e-mail accounts. You have the benefit of consistency if your e-mail address isn't tied to your ISP or your web host. There may come a day when you change ISP's, or you may even move your website to another host. If your e-mail address is tied to either of these, you will have to change your e-mail address on your literature, business cards, website, and any other material that may contain your e-mail address. The benefit of having an e-mail address with Hotmail, Juno, or any of the other free sites, is that your address stays the same no matter where your site is located, and no matter what ISP you may use.

As far as advertising in the physical world, we covered those methods in chapter five, so I hope you read the whole thing. If you've forgotten what those methods are, make sure you re-read that chapter.

OK…did you 'information site' folks read through the above section? I'm not going to repeat it, and there's a lot of stuff up there you needed to read. I'll wait here a moment for any of you that cheated and scanned down to here…

::::::checking watch::::::

Oh…lunchtime…

::::::fixing a sandwich::::::

Where did I put…ah…there they are…

::::::grabbing the pretzels::::::

::::::munch, munch::::::

Oh…yur…weddy…::::::swallow::::::…::::::looking for something to drink ::::::quick::::::

Ah…that's better!

Welcome back. Now where were we? Oh…you 'information site' folks. There are some businesses that simply cannot sell their products over the Internet. At least it's unlikely anyway. A great example is real estate. I'm sure there is probably someone that has purchase real estate online without ever visiting the property, but I'm unaware of it, and I wouldn't count on it becoming commonplace. Does it mean a website has no value if it generates no direct sales? Absolutely not! Even if a site will offer nothing but information about your product or services, it can be a powerful tool for your sales staff. It can provide information about your company, the product or services you offer, and cut down dramatically on the busy work that goes along with selling. Let's take our real estate example for a moment. A couple walks through the door and meets the agent for the first time. They spend 15 minutes or so going over what they are looking for in a home. The agent brings out the MLS books and the hunt begins. They may spend hours going over the books looking for the homes they will go out and see. They may also leave it to the agent to take them around to homes that the agent feels fits the description of what they want. An agent can spend days with the couple going from home to home, hoping that the next one will grab the couple and make them say "This is the one." How much time can be saved, though, when a couple can go through the homes you have to offer from the privacy of their own home? The couple can fill out a questionnaire online, listing what it is they are hoping to find. They can even tag the homes that have caught their eye while they were visiting your site. The agent, having this information before ever meeting the couple, now knows what the couple wants, and has concrete examples of the type of homes the couple likes. This makes the time spent with the couple incredibly efficient and quick, which is so paramount. One of the biggest complaints home seekers have is how long it takes to find the house they want. Often the couple will, after believing they have communicated their wants to the agent effectively, become frustrated because they are seeing homes which have no interest to them. Under the old system, it was often not the fault of the agent; it simply required going to several types of homes to begin to get a feel for what the couple wanted. Most of us are poor at communicating our desires as effectively as we need if we wish to be properly understood by someone else. But when you can point at a picture and say "This," it becomes a very easy thing indeed.

As you build your informative site, you may wish to make yourself into a 'mini-mall' of sorts. Always keep in mind the most important thing to your site is traffic. You have your site up and running, and your real estate company is poised for that phone to start ringing off the hook. In addition to all the things we talked about in the commerce site section preceding (you better have read it), you can make yourself the main site for a cyber mini-mall. You could go out to businesses in your community and recruit them to place pages within your site. What goes better with a real estate site than a local gardening store, or hardware store, swimming pool store, furniture store, grocery store, and on and on. You and the other companies have the benefit of using each other to keep traffic flowing through the site. You, as the 'landlord' have the benefit of making yourself the main home page. By being the opening page, all the traffic will have to flow through your front door before getting to all the other businesses. This will give you tremendous exposure, and is simply a variation on the ad swapping I keep hammering on in this book.

Ad swapping GOOD…going solo BAD…Ugh!

This shouldn't cost any extra above what you would have paid to be alone in your site. You will still be the contact for the web host site. You will simply be selling advertising space on your site to these businesses. Now don't go and try to make a killing from these other businesses. A business site of their own on GeoCities would cost them twenty-five dollars a month, so don't go nuts and try to turn this into a profit center. You need the bulk on your site to keep the traffic flowing. By having bulk, these other companies will be going out and promoting the site also to generate customers for themselves. That means more people pounding the streets promoting your website. So make it cheap, or make it free to the other businesses. They pay for their own page design, but it will be up to you whether or not you charge them…and how much.

In addition to adding other businesses to your site to boost traffic, you can add a chat room. A chat room will enable you to have meetings, seminars, or discussions with customers. Make the chat room available for use by all the businesses sharing your site. Make sure you act as scheduler so there won't be problems between the businesses. The gardening business may bring in a tree expert to conduct a planting and care seminar. Your real estate company may bring in an accountant to go over tax incentives to owning a home. Any topic you or your tenants can think of that will bring people in to the site and generate interest and traffic is beneficial to all of you.

So…as another chapter comes to a close, what are the main things we have learned?

Ackkk!!! Not a quiz?!?!?!

Who said that????? ::::::looking through audience::::::

Yes! A quiz! Now…where was I? Ah!

1. The money truck isn't circling your block waiting for your website to go up so that he can dump money on your front lawn.

2. Swap…Swap…Swap…Swap that advertising! Swap! (just in case you missed it!)

3. Advertise in the virtual and the physical world.

4. Build a site that grabs the viewer from the opening page.

5. Fast response. 24 hours maximum to respond to mail or orders.

6. Constant updates. Your website should change constantly, whether it is specials, new products, or graphics. Internet users tire quickly, so keep them coming back by making your site new for them all the time.

7. Information. Whether it be through chat rooms, newsletters, or pages devoted to topics, Internet users crave information. Become an expert in your business…and the customer will keep coming back to you.

OK…all set for the next chapter…I'll take a peek ahead…Flea markets?????

Eeeeeeewwwwwww…

What can be learned from flea markets??? Hmmmmm…must be something if I included it in the book…so don't pass it. I promise you it will be a fun chapter!!!

CHAPTER NINE

FLEA MARKETS AND ROADSIDE STANDS

Now…wait just a second! Don't go blowing by this chapter because you think you're too dignified to operate a roadside stand or a flea market booth. If you're planning on owning a flea market or roadside business, I want to apologize to you for the people that just tried to skip this chapter! ::::::shaking finger::::::…shame…shame…The flea market and roadside business is one of the most dynamic and interactive that has ever existed. This style of business is where it all started thousands of years ago. The markets in the center of towns spreading all across Europe, Asia, and the Middle East were exciting places. The excitement of this market style is still prevalent in today's flea markets and roadside stands, but they are no longer the primary method by which product is moved through our economy today.

What is it that makes flea markets and roadside stands exciting to so many people? The answer is twofold; it's personal, and it is capitalism at it's best and most fun. The personal style of flea markets and roadside stands is intoxicating to many people. When you pull over to the side of the road to stop at a stand to buy sweet corn, watermelon, or any other produce they may have, you're not buying from some large, faceless corporation. You're buying from the family on whose farm this produce was grown. You get to see them face to face. You know the product wasn't shipped on a truck from somewhere else. You know the produce wasn't picked before it was ripe so that it will be ripe by the time it gets to the store. The produce you see at that stand was picked that morning and is as fresh as Mother Nature can make it. I've seen people bring lawn chairs and just sit at the stands and talk to one another for hours. How many looks would you get at your local grocery store if you brought a lawn chair, set up in aisle 23, and just started talking to people as they pushed their carts by your spot? The same is true for flea markets. Week after week you see the same face at the booth. You develop a personal relationship with the owner of that booth. People stop and carry on conversations and get to know each other, and the atmosphere is very relaxed. I've seen a booth operator yell across the flea market when they see a customer, and tell them about the latest thing they found that the customer might like. It's not uncommon to hear someone shouting across a flea market, "Gladys! Get over here! I got in a pair of those earrings you were talking about last week!" The booth operators know their customers, and their customers know them. Now I'm not talking about 'know' them as in recognition of their face. They really KNOW them. They know their likes, their dislikes, they've talked about family problems, and probably know their life histories. The relationship is a personal one, not just vendor/customer. This personal type of relationship can pay big dividends in any type of business. If you have the space in your store, encourage this community type of atmosphere. Just set up some rocking chairs in an area of the store and give people an opportunity to take a load off of their feet. Make sure you have enough chairs around so that if so inclined, the people may strike up a conversation with each other. You shouldn't hesitate to jump in either. Sit down with them if you are able. Talk to them about no particular topic, or ask them about products for your store. Asking "I was thinking about adding golf balls to the store, do you think that would fly here?" gets them involved. They will feel connected to your store, and to you. Get your customers involved with games at your store. Have charades night, pictionary night, karaoke night, any kind of game or fun activity. Something that makes your store stand out and makes it the fun place to be on a given night. If people come to your store to have fun, they will shop there. One suggestion: if you decide to have a karaoke night, give out prizes for the worst singers. It will free up the reservations people have about singing, and they will be able to laugh at themselves because the idea is to be really bad. If you decide to have game nights, make sure to have prizes. They can be gag gifts, gifts donated as promotions for other businesses (AD SWAP), discounts, or free merchandise from your store. I lean toward (you better get this right) SWAP! Check with local businesses for prizes for your games. A free sandwich at Joe's, or a night's stay at the Blue Moon hotel, etc., all allow you to benefit from the relationships developed with your customers without costing your business a lot of money.

The other thing that makes flea markets and roadside stands fun and exciting is the lost art of haggling over price. There are open-air markets in countries today in which the vendors take great offense if you pay the price they ask for a product. If you have never been to a flea market, go and learn. Take a walk through the aisles, looking and listening intently to the people and your surroundings. Don't just go to one flea market either. Examine each one in your area, learning the nuances that draw these people back time and again. Flea markets are the trenches of marketing. You won't find any business plans, market analysis, pie charts, stock offerings, corporate performance reports, or even one corporate motto here. This is where marketing gets down and dirty, and shines in it's simplest and purest form. If you ignore what there is to learn at a flea market because it is 'beneath you', you will have bypassed an incredible learning experience. One of the most beautiful pieces of music even written was the Adagio of the Clarinet Concerto in A major by Mozart. The most touching, amazing moment in the music is an oboe playing one note by itself. The note is just lingering there waiting to be joined by another. It is one of the most beautiful moments in music, yet is the ultimate in simplicity.

OK…I can hear the groaning already. "I can't believe he's comparing flea markets to Mozart!" That's not the point I was making, and you know it. After all, you've asked such great questions throughout this book. I thought you would have known me better by now…::::::sighs::::::but, alas, I suppose not…

The comparison is that both are elegant in their simplicity. Marketing boils down to one thing…getting someone to pay a price for your product that will generate a profit to you, thereby allowing you to pay your bills. Businesses can cloud that one simple reality, and begin to live for reports rather than for profits. I can guarantee you that a person at a flew market never loses sight of that one reality. They simply look at a product that costs them one dollar and know that when they've sold it for three dollars, they made a profit of two dollars. Simple, unadulterated 'sell your product at a profit' marketing. No bells, no whistles. If you have the time and inclination, I would even suggest you open a booth at a flea market for a month or two just to get into the trenches and learn some of the techniques of some of the more successful booth operators. If you immerse yourself and learn the art of haggling, you will have a great deal of fun. I operated a booth over the weekends for several months in preparation for this book. There was one gentleman that I would consider the King of the flea marketers. I was fortunate that my booth was close to his, and I got to listen to his daily interaction with his customers. He would average around two thousand dollars a day, while the average daily take for a booth owner was a few hundred dollars. Why did his customers keep coming back week after week…and spending so much money? As with any business, some things take time. He had built up regular clientele over the years. He knew them personally, their likes and dislikes, and knew them by their first names on sight. With a regular client base in tow, he had begun years before to change his inventory every week. All his clients knew they needed to get to him ever week, because they just never knew when they might find their own little treasure. He had his two hooks...'Get here every week or you'll miss out,' and he was inexpensive. He was also a master of the art of haggling, and his repartee was an absolute pleasure to get to listen to each week. The banter was typical, but always fun. A customer would hold up an object and ask about the price. He might say two dollars...to which the customer would fire back "I'll give you one dollar." The gentleman would reply, "You're killing me! Just takin' the food right out of my kids' mouths!" Then he'd reach for his wallet and say, "Here, you may as well just take it all, cause you're robbin' me here!" Then the selling kicked in to high gear. "I'll tell you what," he'd say. "I'll sell that to you for a dollar, but at the little bit of nothin' I'm making, I'll sell you this and this." By the time he was done with her, she had purchased about twenty dollars worth of merchandise, when she was only planning on buying the one item...for one dollar. The art of leading people by allowing them to lead is one that more people should develop. This gentleman knew exactly which items to add to her one item because he had been paying attention to the items in which she had shown interest. With this information, it was an easy nudge to get her to purchase the items along with her one item. He let her lead him to the products she wanted, and he, after nudging her in the right direction, followed her to the purchase. Absolutely elegant in it's simplicity!

Whether or not you go to a flea market to walk down the aisles or to run a booth for a while, go there as a student. Watch, listen, and learn. On average, the booth operators will be some of the nicest people you have ever met. They help each other, watch booths for one another, and even collect money for you if you're not there. Most are more than willing to talk freely, so ask them plenty of questions. From them you will learn 'in the trenches' marketing in it's purest form. Treasure the experience and incorporate it into your business. Learn to haggle, whether you open a booth or not. It will really help with your negotiation techniques, and you will have a lot of fun at the same time. So what do you do if you decide to try flea markets for a time? Most likely the business you wish to eventually operate won't be suited to a flea market. First you need to decide what type of market you wish to try.

1. Roadside stands—If you wish to do this temporarily, for the learning experience, I wouldn't recommend a roadside stand. Whatever product you decide to sell, you will not have anyone from whom to learn. A roadside stand operator looks for a street corner or a vacant lot, and sets up his wares. It's you and your goods, and that's all. You also have to hope that the owner of the vacant lot doesn't find out you're there, and have you kicked off his property. If you set up on a sidewalk, you have to hope the police don't drive by and move you along on your way. If you decide to try it anyway, make sure you get permission to set up on the property. And no black velvet Elvis paintings! I can't tell you how many times I've driven down a road and seen a roadside stand with black velvet Elvis paintings. It must be something in the roadside stand bylaws.

2. Festivals—The strongest sales time in an indoor flea market is the winter. Warm weather typically equals lousy sales in an indoor flea market. This means that a lot of year 'round flea market merchants need to go to where the action is in the late spring through early fall. That place is festivals and fairs. At a fair or festival you'll typically find two types of merchants; summer merchants and year 'round merchants. The summer merchants tend to be flea market people in the winter, whereas the year 'round merchants travel the festivals all year long. That means they spend a large portion of the year living like nomads, following the weather, moving north in the summer, and heading south as the seasons cool. If you wish to participate in the fairs and festivals with a booth, it's easy. Just contact your state for a visitor's guide to the fairs and festivals in your state. That guide will list the contact person that can give you the necessary information to

be able to open a booth at a fair festival. Keep in mind though that for a learning experience (although it is better than roadside stands), you won't necessarily be in close proximity to another vendor. Fairs and festivals can often cover a large number of acres, which can make it difficult to spend time with your fellow vendors.

3. Flea markets—There are two types of flea markets; indoor and outdoor. Outdoor flea markets are made up largely of people that brought all their junk from their garage, and are praying that someone will buy it so that they don't have to deal with it anymore. Indoor vendors are more often the ones that do this either as a supplemental or primary source of income. As I said before, the cool months are the strongest time for indoor flea markets. The general rule of thumb is that if it's a nice day to be outside, the customers won't be inside to see you. November to March is typically the strong time for an indoor flea market. Here you will have the proximity that will allow you to learn from your fellow vendors.

If, however, you wish to do the flea market/festival business full time, you'll need to know where you're going to get product. The first thing you need to decide is new or old? If you're going to sell used product, you need to keep an eye out for product. As morbid as it may sound, you can keep an eye on obituaries. If you notice someone who died and was living alone, contact the family…after allowing for a proper time of mourning. The remaining family will often go through the personal effects and remove possessions of monetary or personal value. Often, however, there is a great deal of goods left behind. More often than not, the family contacts a charity that will come and collect the goods and be done with it. If you can make arrangements, you can often negotiate a purchase price for the remaining goods. It will typically net you a truckload or more of goods for very little.

You will also want to make the garage sale rounds. Most people run a garage sale Thursday through Saturday. If so, go on Thursday, before it opens, and check out their goods. If you see several good things, then make an offer to take everything off of their hands. Even if there are things you don't want, make the offer to take it all. This will dramatically cut your cost per item, because the person will not be thinking price per item, but of the whole dollar amount. I can safely say that most places you go, if you offer them one hundred dollars to take it all, will jump at the chance, rather than have to box the leftovers again.

If you wish to sell new items, you need to find your niche and your supplier(s). Most cities of any size will have wholesalers in town that sell novelty items. Novelty items are easy to get and easy to sell. They cost very little, so you can double or triple your unit cost and still be very cheap at the flea market. If you wish to do something different than novelty toys, you need to find your niche. Always remember though, people that patronize a flea market are looking for the deal. If your merchandise is cheap, then you have no problem. If you merchandise is not cheap, you need to make them feel as if they are getting one incredible deal. You can do this by marking the price up and then marking it back down. Electronics stores and jewelry stores are famous for taking this practice to the max. Have you ever heard of an electronics store that wasn't running a sale? Try to get the customer to tell you what a fair price would be for the item. Often they will offer more than the price you would have been willing to take for the item. Or, it can give you the chance to use the 'you're killing me' routine and haggle yourself silly.

Got your quiz paper ready? There are two main things you should have pulled out of this chapter…

::::::humming the Jeopardy music::::::

I see someone writing…so that's good…

Ah…you…yes…you…get to writing…and quit looking on his paper.

Ready?

Pencils down…

Pencils down…

Hey! Stop it! Pencils down already!

The two things were ::::::drumroll::::::

1. Get to know your customers intimately. Their needs, wants, names, etc.

2. Make the customer's experience with you a fun one. Keep them interested…so that they keep coming back.

OK…all done…move on…turn the page…Chapter 10…here we come!

CHAPTER TEN

▼

COLLECTIBLES

If you're thinking of opening a business that has to do with collectibles grab onto something and get ready for a serious addiction. It doesn't matter if you're going to sell beanies, ballcards, diecast, figurines, toys, coins, stamps, or any of the myriad of items people collect, you will get hooked, and hooked fast. I must admit of all the businesses I've owned this is the one I would keep even if it was a money loser. This chapter originally was never planned to be a part of the book. As I was doing a holiday show as research for the retail chapter of this book I was misled by a promoter when I rented space for his show. Since it was the holiday season I took a good bit of toy merchandise from the store and headed off to another mall to sell the merchandise at rented tables for a mall show. Most of you have most likely been to your local mall when they have had a special show. Down the center of the mall aisles will be table after table of merchandise according to what type of show is in the mall that weekend. When I told the promoter the type of merchandise I had for sale he stated it was a toy show. It turned out to be a ballcard show. Needless to say I learned quickly you don't take merchandise to a show that doesn't fit. If you're going to a ballcard show, you won't be selling many toys. After I had been there for an hour or so I didn't mind the deception on the part of the promoter. The people with whom I was surrounded were fascinating. Listening to them talk to customers and one another was an education I was enjoying beyond measure. On the second day of the three day show I decided this segment of the retail business was so distinctive as to warrant it's own separate chapter. I then went around to each of the dealers and started trading my merchandise for ballcards like a madman. The thing you will find at ballcard shows is that trading is almost like a drug to collectors. The art of doing the trade so that you feel as if you walked away with a sweet deal. It only took one day for me to do enough trading so that by the end of the show I was the proud owner of over 100,000 ballcards. Did it cost me a fortune in product to gain ownership of that many cards? In truth, it cost me about four hundred dollars worth of product and about fifty dollars in cash. When a dealer is near the end of the show and is looking around at the boxes that will have to be loaded back into the car, it's amazing the deals another dealer can get. For the astronomical amount of four hundred and fifty dollars I was now the owner of nearly $50,000 worth of ballcards according to their book value. So I set off to learn all I could from the people that were in the business, by plunging into the business myself. I must admit, it has been a fun ride while writing this chapter. The conversations I had with customers and dealers were much more intimate. You talk to people about their interests as if you had known them for a long time. The item they are collecting and you are selling forms a bond between the two of you. The personal nature of collecting was one that went far beyond retail. The items people collect have intimate meaning to them, connecting you to the customer in a way that selling them a shirt or a toaster never could. When a person decides to collect a particular type of item or memorabilia they form an emotional bond with these inanimate objects. They form this bond with objects because it gives them a feeling of connection to the person, time, or place to which the objects relate. The level of emotional attachment is also directly related to the number and value of the objects the person collects. The range of customers will encompass the entire spectrum. Starting with the fan who sees an inexpensive item they can buy as a memento of their home team. And ending with the person you see on television that has an entire house full of Elvis memorabilia, including towels containing Elvis sweat, and hair clippings that were guaranteed to be real Elvis hair by that honest guy from the 'Elvis is living on the planet Venus' newsletter. Extremes are something present in all walks of life. Although the vast majority of collectors get great enjoyment from their hobby, there are those on either ends of the spectrum that tend to make it very colorful. On one end you have the people that ridicule anyone that collects memorabilia as being stupid. Ironically those that collect will tend to ridicule the objects that others collect. The jabs can especially run rampant between sports collectors and beanie collectors. I've seen people who sell ballcards and diecast lean back in their chair and say, "What idiot would collect beanies?" Keep in mind the person is saying this surrounded by his ballcards and his metal racing cars. I've also heard beanie collectors say the same thing about sports collectors when the beanies are so much cuter than, 'a silly old piece of cardboard.' Someone said, "Anyone that drives slower than me is an idiot, and anyone that drives faster than me is a moron." Collectors seem to think the same way. 'Anything I collect has value, anything you collect is just silly.'

In the next several pages we're going to take a look at the various types of dealers, stores, and marketing possibilities as well as the different types of customers you will encounter in the collectibles business. We will also examine how you can create the emotional attachment between your business and the customer that collectibles dealers enjoy, regardless of the type of business you intend to start. Now before we get started I want you to admit it, you've got something stashed away up in your closet don't you? Come on, we're all friends here. You've got something in there that you collect or collected when you were a kid. Or was your mother like so many and threw out your baseball cards when she felt you had gotten too old for them? Want to know how much they would be worth today? Believe me, you don't want to know. That's my only regret about getting into this business to research this chapter. I now know what the cards are worth that Mom threw out lo those years ago.

Within the collectibles business we will examine five basic types of collectibles dealers. Each has a different approach and impact upon the business. Knowing the various approaches up front will allow you to plan which approach is best for you, and how to succeed against each approach. Before plunging into the world of collectibles however, let's brush up on the lingo that is so uniquely theirs. If you can't speak the language you will feel as if you've taken a vacation in Italy and forgotten your English to Italian dictionary. We will use ballcards for our example since they are the most colorful. A great deal of the lingo however transfers from collectible to collectible.

Hobby: These are the versions of the cards that are worth the money. The hobby versions are carried by sports card stores, and not by retail stores. Hobby cards tend to be a bit thicker, of higher quality, and usually have the hotter cards such as autographs. Some retail packs carry autographs, but not many. Dealers and true collectors tend to look down their noses at the retail cards and the people that buy them. There is no distinction on the card as to whether it is a retail card or a hobby card. You gain the ability to recognize the differences with experience. Sometimes the differences are distinct because the retail and hobby versions are completely different designs. If that is the case you simply need learn which is which. You can often learn the difference between design versions by looking in the Beckett pricing guide. When they list a main category of a card they will often show a picture of the card. The picture shown is always the hobby version. If the hobby and retail design is the same, the only way to tell is by comparing the quality and thickness of the card.

Retail: Not wanting to miss a market most of the card manufacturers make a retail version of their cards. The card manufacturers are aware of the fact that more people walk through retail stores such as Wal-Mart than through their local sports card stores. The question was how to tap into that market without alienating the very lucrative hobby trade. The answer was a retail version of the hobby card. Retail boxes of packs will often have a different number of packs per box, different number of cards per pack, and be of slightly lesser quality and thickness. It is a very good rule of thumb in the trade that a retail card has fifty percent of the value of the hobby version of the card. The casual buyer strolling through their local Wal-Mart doesn't know that though. Shoppers will often pay more per card for retail versions than they would for hobby versions. The reason is standard retailer markups. If a box costs a retailer thirty dollars, the retail price will most likely be sixty dollars, if they have a standard fifty percent margin markup. The hobby box may cost the hobby store fifty dollars, but the hobby store knows the level of action for that particular box so he may only mark it up to seventy dollars. The casual shopper that knows nothing of the trade will compare the price of the boxes at sixty dollars retail or seventy dollars hobby and buy the retail box. The shopper doesn't bother to see that the retail box contains thirty packs of five cards each versus the hobby box of thirty-six packs of eight cards each. As a result the shopper paid sixty dollars for one hundred and fifty retail cards versus seventy dollars for two hundred and eighty-eight cards. The hobby cards, worth twice as much as their retail counterparts, cost twenty-four cents per card versus forty cents per card for the retail version.

Wax Packs: Although the packs that contain the cards are now as nearly high tech as the cards inside, they were once made of wax paper. In the old days of cards (prior to the early 1990's), wax paper was used to protect the cards inside from moisture, hence the name wax packs. The term still is used though it is no longer accurate.

Poppin Wax: The phrase 'poppin wax' is used to describe the moment when you open the pack containing the cards. In the old days you simply hoped when you opened a pack your favorite player would be inside. Sometimes you hoped that you would get a duplicate of a certain card you already had so that you could trade Jimmy down the street for his Hank Aaron card that you really wanted. Those days are long gone. Now opening a pack is often like buying a scratch-off lottery ticket. You grab the pack firmly between your hands, dig the finger of one hand down into the seam, separate the two sides from one another, pull out the cards inside, and shuffle through them slowly hoping to get a big card. With cards that have a book price of twenty thousand dollars or more it has become quite the different business it was even ten short years ago. Long gone are the days where a card manufacturer simply put cards of the players from a team onto the market for the public. Now there are short runs, numbered cards, autographed cards, holograms, motion cards, pop-up cards, inserts, and the list goes on and on.

Wax Addict: This is someone who is hooked on opening wax packs. These people have many of the obsessive characteristics of someone with a gambling addiction. Some addicts have the money to indulge their obsession, many wax addicts do not however. These are the people that will spend money they can't afford always thinking the next pack will have the monster card that will make a lot of money. The problem is one of using the correct numbers. When the wax junkie hits a big card they begin to have selective memory. The wax junkie will smile with glee telling everyone how he popped a card worth five hundred dollars out of a pack that cost him four dollars. Initially the math sounds very good. He lays four dollars on the counter and in the moment it takes to open the pack he is holding a card worth five hundred dollars in his hand. The selective memory comes into play when he ignores the thousands of dollars spent prior to that four dollars. Wax junkies always lose money. Much like scratch off lottery tickets it is a numbers game. If you play one scratch off lottery ticket and hit big, you are way ahead of the game. If however, you take your winnings and buy more scratch off tickets the odds will catch up with you and all your winnings will be gone. The distinction between someone opening wax packs for profit and a wax junkie is very much akin to the difference between a compulsive gambler and a professional gambler. The professional when opening wax packs does so based upon the action a certain brand of cards is getting at the time and the profit he believes can be made from the cards. The professional is also buying the boxes of wax packs at wholesale or mid-retail prices, resulting in a lower per card price. The professional buying at wholesale prices also has the ability to sell wax packs. This ability allows them to purchase a case of product wholesale, open half of the wax packs for single cards, and sell the other half of the wax packs. The profit from the wax packs sold pays for the wax packs opened, resulting in his no money invested in the single cards. One wax addict in particular that I have seen loses upwards of thirty thousand dollars per year to his addiction. He knows it, can afford it, and enjoys it, so it's not a problem for him. He rents table space at the occasional show and sells the cards at blowout prices. Selling the cards at shows at regular intervals gives him the ability to write his addiction off on his taxes. As a dealer you will only recognize a wax addict if he or she becomes a regular customer of yours. If you recognize them as an addict and you know their financial situation can not afford their habits, talk to them. This is a wonderful hobby and is a tremendous amount of fun. Don't knowingly take advantage of someone's addiction and by continuing to sell product to them at their detriment. If you want to be a healthy part of the community sometimes it means looking out for your customers above your bank account. If you wish to look more long term, a serious wax junkie will bankrupt themselves opening wax packs. If they do that you won't have a customer. Teaching them how to enjoy their hobby, rather than become obsessed with it, will help you both in the long run.

Base Set: In each type of card there is a base set. This is the set that will represent the majority of the cards within the wax packs for that type of card. The base set can run anywhere from one hundred to over eight hundred cards. Mixed in the packs with the base cards could be inserts, short runs, numbered cards, autographed cards, or any other type of specialty card created by the manufacturer.

Short Run: This term is rather self-explanatory. In a set of cards the manufacturer will decide how many sets he will manufacture. If that number is ten thousand, then there will be ten thousand of each card within the base set made and randomly inserted into wax packs. Sometimes there will be less made of a particular card within that set. It can be by design as an attempt to create interest, or there could have been a problem in manufacturing the card. Being on a strict timetable, if cards are damaged and destroyed at the manufacturer they are rarely replaced. This will create a short count on one or more of the players in the set. How many were destroyed will determine how short that card will be and as a result how much it is worth. It will create an artificial demand for the card because people trying to put together an entire set of the cards will have a harder time finding the card.

Numbered Cards: These are the hot items today in the sports card industry. When you look at the card printed on the front or the back will be, for example, #97 of 100. That number would mean that only one hundred of those cards were printed. If you have one in your hand it would mean that there were only ninety-nine others in the entire world. Numbered cards vary in value primarily according to how many, and whose picture is on the card. The truly sought after numbered cards are the cards that are 1 of 1. When you hold that you have something truly special because it is the only one of it's kind in the world. Even common players can be worth two hundred dollars or more. A 1 of 1 card of a hot player can be worth many thousands of dollars.

Autographed Cards: When certified and placed in packs by the manufacturer, these cards can be quite valuable. Value is determined by the number of cards autographed by the player, and the popularity of the player. Cards that are personally autographed are a hard sell. Most dealers will not buy them from customers, and dealers can get very little for them from their customers. The reason is rampant forgery. As in any industry there are people that are liars and thieves. These people will take cards and other memorabilia and sign the name of the player and sell it as genuine. Unless the autographed item is accompanied by a certificate of authenticity that is signed by a recognized verification agency, you are better off not purchasing the item. If you purchase an autograph item for resale to a customer and the autograph is found to a forgery, it is your reputation that is damaged. If you have built a trust between yourself and the customer then often customers will feel comfortable buying items that you have had autographed by an athlete or star. If you were physically there and watched the athlete sign the item it will make your customers comfortable that the signature is indeed genuine. If there was a charge to have the item signed you will often receive a ticket for the autograph. Save the ticket and include it with the autographed item when it is sold. You may also create a certificate of authenticity stating that you witnessed the signature and guarantee the signature to be authentic. This certificate will carry little official weight, but by placing your signature to a guarantee it will make the customer feel more comfortable.

Hard Hit: A hard hit is a card that is very simply a rare card. Most wax packs have the pull ratios listed on the back of each pack. The pull ratios tell you just how hard it is to hit a particular type of insert. For example the pack may state Hologram Cards 1:700. This means that the hologram cards in that series are randomly distributed at an average of one card out of every seven hundred packs of cards. That would be a very hard hit considering boxes of cards contain anywhere from a dozen to forty-eight packs of cards. The mathematics is very simple, the harder the hit the more valuable the card.

Searched: This is a very shady practice and one that thankfully the manufacturers have made more difficult. It was often the case, before the manufacturers caught on to this practice, that inserts and special cards could be of a different thickness, a different color along the edge, or some distinguishing characteristic that could be seen or felt while the pack was still sealed. In addition it was often the case that the wax packs themselves were either clear or semi-transparent along the edge. With the combination of these two factors unscrupulous dealers and customers were able to figure out which packs contained the valuable cards. The dishonest dealers would then remove the valuable packs from the boxes and sell the remainder of the packs to customers. The customers would buy hoping they would hit cards that had already been removed. It was also possible in the old wax days to actually open the packs, search it, and then seal it shut again. All it would require was a little heat to allow the wax coating to become soft enough for the folds to stick together again.

Dealers would many times have the problems with customers as well. While a dealer would have his back turned, a customer would rummage through the box trying to find the packs containing the hot cards, leaving the remaining packs for the other customers. This led to the practice of dealers putting boxes out of reach of the customer. This way when a customer wanted to purchase packs the dealer would by necessity be there to ensure that the customer wasn't searching the packs. The dealer shouldn't go so far as to take away the superstitions of the customer however. Some customers have told me that the manufacturers always put hot cards in the fourth pack from the top, or the third pack from the bottom on the right side of the box. It's amazing how some customers think they have cracked the manufacturer code. The truth is that the packs that contain the hot cards are placed in the boxes completely at random. The customers are fun to watch though as they try for the big card. The best thing you can do is to shake your head in agreement and wish them luck.

Book: Beckett is the price guide that is the standard in the industry. There are other price guides for ballcards but they are not used as a standard by dealers and collectors so you won't be able to use them effectively to price your product. Beckett publishes a price guide for each sport, as well as a price guide for figurines, racing merchandise, and various collectibles. Each guide has a set day each month it is released, giving a constant weekly flow of price guides rather than a glut at the first of each month. When you open a Beckett price guide the prices of the cards are listed in a range from low to high. Most dealers price at the high Beckett price and then discount from there. High Beckett, as it is called, is referred to as book price. The low end of the price range listed is called Low Beckett. You will learn as you talk with other dealers how strong or weak your local market is in regard to pricing. Some states have a strong market, allowing you to charge near or at full book price. Some states have a weaker market, forcing you to sell at half Beckett. Half Beckett is fifty percent off of the high Beckett price. If you open your store in a half Beckett state don't be discouraged. Even at half Beckett there are still wonderful profits to be made. You must also know your product. Even if a store sells their cards at half Beckett, they don't necessarily sell all of their cards at half Beckett. Some sell rookie cards, numbered, cards, autographed cards, and so on at a price between high Beckett and half Beckett.

Making Table: Whether it's called making table or making rent it is a term dealers use to know when they have started working for themselves at either their store or at a show. If a dealer has rented two tables at a show at a cost of one hundred dollars he will track his profits and once he has made a profit of one hundred dollars he will know that he has made table, or paid the rent so to speak. After making table he knows the remainder of the profits are his. Dealers will often compare notes on shows and the common line they will use to compare shows is how fast they made their table. If a dealer is doing a three-day show and on the third day he has yet to make table, often the dealer will not only not do that show again, he will let other dealers know how bad a show it was as well. Most dealers will want to make their table the first day of a three-day show so that days two and three are their days. Making table can also be referred to as 'working for the promoter'. A dealer may say, "I worked for Dave Friday, and the other two days were for me." A dealer with a storefront will often track to find which day each month he pays for the rent of the store.

Make Me Sweet: This is a colorful term used in negotiating trades with people who walk into your store or walk by your table at a show. Over time you will develop your own style when it comes to trading. Trading cards is a very valuable tool because often you can trade to get cards you know you can sell. You can also use trading to increase the value of your inventory without an exchange of cash for product. A good rule to live by is that you rarely, unless the deal is just too incredible to pass, want to trade your autographs, numbered cards, or hot rookies for the cards a customer will bring to you. Other than that enjoy. Trading can be a tremendous amount of fun. If you are at a show and a customer walks by your table and wishes to do some trading, they will have brought cards they are willing to trade to you. You will go through their cards and pick out the one you would have interest in obtaining from them. If you've been in the business a few years you'll have in your head a ballpark price of what the cards are worth. For the rest of us there is the handy-dandy price guide. Let's say you've selected cards that have a book price of one hundred dollars out of the cards the customer offered to you. You would then ask them what they were wanting for the cards. If they pick out one hundred dollars worth of cards you would be doing a straight exchange for even money. Your one-hundred dollars worth of cards for his one-hundred dollars worth of cards. Unless he's giving you an autograph or a numbered card, it is most likely not a deal you would wish to conduct. If you have a standard percentage of trade tell him what it is. You may trade at eighty percent. That means that one-hundred dollars worth of his cards would get eighty dollars worth of your cards. If your customer has some questions about that then you would say, "Hey, I'm paying rent on these tables to be here. I can't trade even or I'm losing money. If you want to trade to get those cards you're going to have to make me sweet here." Most customers understand that and have no problem with the concept of trading at a lesser value because of your overhead.

Action: This is simply a term used to describe the level of sales activity for a product, or a player. If a dealer has a lot of action on Manning, you know he sells a lot of Peyton Manning cards. If a dealer tells you his wax had no action at a particular show, you know that he sold little, if any, wax packs at the show.

Cherry Picking: When you buy sports figurines from a manufacturer you buy boxes of the merchandise. In those boxes will be figurines that will sell quickly, some that will sell at an acceptable pace, and some that will take longer to sell than it does for a politician to tell the truth. Other dealers or some customers will want to cherry pick the hot players from the boxes and leave you with the players no one wants. Stores such as Wal-Mart that are not in the card business put out this merchandise and have clearance sales praying to get rid of the other players. They can get away with this practice because once the price drops to a low enough level, someone will purchase the unwanted player as a toy to be used and abused. Dealers, not having that luxury, will need to price the merchandise so that the medium action, and hot action players will not only pay for the entire box of figurines, but for his profit as well. By pricing the figurines according to how heavy the action is on the player you guarantee your profit on the box. You also can look at the unwanted items and, having no money in them any longer, dump them off on another dealer at pennies on the dollar and feel good about doing it.

Cream: This term is used to describe the high priced cards. Cream is usually considered to be a card that has a value of fifty dollars or higher. I believe it is safe to assume the term came about as a result of a shortening of the phrase pertaining to cream rising to the top.

Baby Cards: Unless you have a lot of money to sink into cards this is the level at which most dealers start. Baby cards are the low-end cards worth less than fifty dollars. A dealer may refer to a show at which a lot of low priced cards sell as a 'baby show.' Like wise a show at which primarily high priced cards sell will be referred to as a 'cream show.' Most dealers will carry a lot of cream and some baby cards so that they don't lose out on the cheap end of the market at a show. As a new dealer, you will more than likely start out selling primarily baby cards and through trading, popping, and buy-outs, raise the level and value of your cards toward the higher end.

Cut Throat Show: These are shows every dealer dreads. There will be times when one dealer decides to blow a show for everyone and drop their

prices into the toilet. Thankfully ballcards are little affected when someone decides to blow-out their product. Beanie baby dealers are horribly
affected by cut-throat dealers however. While beanie babies cost a dealer
the same regardless of retired status they are sold by their book value. The
book value of the beanies is determined by how many were produced,
whether they are retired, and so on. A cut-throat dealer will set-up at a
show and blow-out all his beanies at the same price. Generally that price
can be as low as six dollars. The cut-throat dealer will be satisfied to make
two to three dollars per beanie, even if the book value on an item is
twenty, thirty, forty dollars or higher. It is not a terribly intelligent business practice. The volume that must be sold to compensate for the lost
margin is enormous. Once a cut-throat dealer is in full swing at a show the
value of the beanies in the eyes of the customer is immediately gone.
Customers start going from table to table shopping price, and low bidder
wins. The other beanie dealers can match the price, or hold firm and hope
the low priced dealers sell-out quickly. Either way it represents a lose-lose
situation for the dealers. The reason sports card dealers are relatively unaf-
fected is that the dealers are at the show before the customers arrive. When
a dealer is going to set-up at a show and price his cards at blow-out prices,
the other dealers will swarm over his product and purchase most of the
cards of value. If a dealer sells at half-book and has the opportunity to pick
up some nice cards at ten to twenty percent book he stands to profit by
purchasing the cards. By purchasing the cards he gives himself an opportunity to make a profit on the cards, and he also removes stock from the
blow-out dealer that could be competition to his own stock. It also allows
the dealer a nice response if someone should question why he is selling at
half-book, when the other dealer is selling at twenty-percent book. The
dealer can look him honestly in the eye and say, "He doesn't have anything
that anybody would want over there." As a result card dealers actually like
to see a blow-out dealer now and then. It's a nice feeling to buy a two-hun-
dred dollar card from a blow-out dealer for twenty dollars prior to the
show opening, and sell it later that day for one-hundred dollars. Beanie

dealers can't do that. If you're paying three dollars each for your stock, you have no incentive to buy a blow-out dealers stock at six dollars each.

Every business has it's unique terminology and twists on words. To communicate effectively they are terms you will need to learn and given time will become comfortable in their usage.

As we had begun to discuss, there are five basic types of dealers in the collectible business. You will need to decide which approach will work the best for you and what it is you wish to accomplish. It will also behoove you (yes, I did say behoove and won't my Grandfather be proud I did) to know all the types of dealers so that you can not only compete effectively, but know from whom to buy product and when.

The Collector: This individual is not in the business to make money. They often are trying to find particular players, teams, or sets and pop a lot of wax to accomplish that goal. By doing this they generate a lot of cards that they do not wish to keep. Being worth money they will not simply throw them away. They will sell the cards to recover some of the money they have spent. Recovering this money will allow them more funds to buy more wax packs, giving them more unwanted cards that they will sell. I think you get the idea. It's a cycle for them that will continue as long as they wish to collect cards. These individuals will rent table space at the occasional show and tend to blow-out their cards at cheap prices. These are dealers it will be in your interest to find before the show opens to the public. You can get some wonderful deals from them on cards that will turn a nice profit for you. You may also be able to strike a private deal with them to go through their cards a week or two before they are considering the possibility of doing a show. If they are willing, get their contact information and tell them that before they do another show to call you. If you buy enough of their product they may decide to not do a show. If this is the case you will have found your own private source of some very nice product. The best way to compete with this type of dealer at a show is to hold your prices at the level that is normal for you. Don't cheapen your material to keep up with them, you will lose. They are not there to make a profit. Their desire is to recover some of the money they have already spent so that they can buy more wax. To compete with them simply go through their merchandise before the show and buy the valuable cards for your inventory.

The Weekend Warrior: These are the dealers who rent tables at shows nearly every weekend. Some do it as their primary source of income, and some do it for extra money up and above their paycheck. It's a rowdy and fun bunch. If you do shows for any length of time at all you will get to know this bunch very well. Often it is nearly the same set of dealers at each show. Some will be willing to travel further than others, but often there will be a circuit of shows at which everyone rents space. When you first start doing shows, talk to as many of the dealers as you can. They will be more than happy to fill you in on the good shows and the bad shows. If you decide to do weekend shows on a regular basis, invest in a good hand cart. You will be moving your product into the show site and trying to get set-up in under two hours. You will most certainly not want to carry your product in by hand. You will also want a hand cart that can carry as much product as possible. The fewer trips you must make in and out of the site the better. Unlike a storefront you will be moving your product in and then moving it back out within a short span of time. Some shows are one day, some are two days, and some are three days. Your inventory will need to be easily transportable and stackable. You will learn who, as you do more and more shows, on the circuits are good promoters. Once you have identified the promoters who advertise their shows and can draw a good crowd, the best thing is to work with two or three and stick with their circuits. There are a lot of show promoters in the industry and most simply promote shows to get free space for their own merchandise. As with most anything in this world you get what you pay for. If you see that a promoter is holding a show and is only charging twenty or thirty dollars to rent a table, you can bet it's not being advertised. Cheap table rent equals little traffic and a promoter who has his own regular customers and using your table rent so that he can sell his merchandise for free.

Storefront: One of the perks to opening a collectibles store is that if you develop a loyal following you don't necessarily need to be in a high traffic, hence expensive, mall or strip mall. Even out of the way collectibles stores can be successful if, and I repeat if, they take care of their customers. Collectibles customers tend to be fiercely loyal to the person with which they do business. As long as you do your best for your customer in supplying them product, treating them fairly on sales and trades, and helping them to find the items they wish to buy, they will stick with you like glue. This fierce loyalty will snowball as your happy customers tell their other friends about how well you take care of them. Once you have a storefront you will be able to purchase boxes of wax packs directly from the manufacturers. They will require that you send them photographs of your business, a copy of your merchant license, proof of ownership, and other standard information. You will be happily surprised when you discover the markups on wax boxes and the profit to be made. You will easily be able to pay for any wax packs you open with the profits from the wax packs that you sell. The amount of markup though will vary upon the action that the particular series receives. You will also be stunned just how many different card series and card manufacturers are out there. You will not be able, or even want, to carry them all. By doing shows before taking the step to own a storefront, and checking the prices each month in your Beckett price guides you will be able to identify the packs you need to carry in your inventory. Having opened a storefront you will also need to be able to provide supplies to your customers. As people collect cards, beanies, helmets, magazines, or anything else you can think to collect, they need a way to protect them. Hard sleeves, display cases, boxes, folders, ball holders, and so on all represent a very lucrative profit center. Regardless of which player is hot, or which sport is seeing a lot of action, the collector will always need supplies to protect their collectibles. The actual collectible market is very volatile. You're constantly riding the wave and trying to keep ahead of the changing appetites of your customers. The supplies end however is a constant. A hard sleeve designed to protect a card doesn't care which player it's protecting.

Make your storefront a valuable part of the community. If you sell ball-cards, sponsor a little league team. Make ballcards of the local high school or little league team players. Arrange to have local police or firemen to come to your store and talk to kids about safety. If you have a professional sports team in your town make friendships with one or more of the players and ask them to come to your store to sign autographs for your customers. The only limit to the number of ways to bring people into your store is your imagination. Collecting is an activity you want your customers to enjoy for a lifetime. The best way to do that is to develop close ties with the children in your community. If you cultivate in those children a devotion and loyalty to your store, that devotion and loyalty will stay with them as adults.

Storefront/Dealer: Although a person that opens a storefront selling collectibles can develop a loyal following over time, the question becomes one of getting people there in the first place. You will also lose customers to natural attrition, regardless of how loyal they are to your store. People move away, new people move to town, or they may lose interest in collecting. For any business to maintain the volume of business conducted they must at least replace customers at the rate at which they are lost. An excellent way of doing this is to rent tables at collectibles shows. By doing this you expose yourself to a customer base that may not be familiar with your store. Always make sure to take along plenty of business cards. Pass them out to anyone and everyone that stops by your table. As you talk to them about what they are trying to find, use the opportunity to talk up your store. The majority of people that rent tables at mall shows are storefront owners. They will rarely do hotel shows for one big reason, traffic. Hotel shows tend to draw a small number of high-end buyers. Storefront owners prefer to do mall shows because they want to use the show to draw people into their store. There is the rare show that has the ability to generate such huge sales that a storefront owner will rent tables simply for the money. Once a show gets beyond the drawing distance from your store your motivation for doing a show must change. No longer will store promoting be an option or possible reward. Once you are outside of that radius the decision to do the show becomes straight dollars and cents. Those shows are not common and will take a lot of trial and error on your part to find them if you wish to seek them out. Your fellow dealers will be your best source of information as to where these mega-dollar shows are located.

Storefront/Promoter: As a storefront owner you may also take the route of sponsoring a show or multiple shows. In addition to promoting shows to gain customers for your own store, you can promote several shows across a particular geography as it's own profit center. If you are promoting a show to drive customers to your storefront you will only want to promote a show on your home turf. By promoting your own local show you can use your store to drive people into the show. This helps to tie your customers closer to you because you are helping them to find items you may not necessarily have in your store. By exposing them to new dealers you keep the activity of collecting fresh to them. If the activity stays exciting and fresh they will stay customers much longer. Some storefront owners won't promote a local show because they consider the dealers at the show to be competitors. This concept is very shallow and not well though out. The dealers at the show are not people you are forced to compete with on a daily basis. They come in for one or two days for the scheduled show, sell their goods, and they go home. The time they compete directly with you is minimal, and the long term good they can do for your store far outweighs the slight amount of competition they offer. The dealers also offer you a wonderful opportunity for new product for your store. Every dealer has product that moves slowly or not at all. If you check with them, they will happily direct you to their slow moving product. As you examine the product you may find things that you are confident would sell in your store. The combination of you being able to move the product, and the dealer being motivated to unload slow moving product is a wonderful thing to behold. Both you and the dealer will walk away happy. The dealer will have converted non-moving product into cash, and you will have purchased product for pennies on the dollar that you know will sell in your store. Dealers are what I refer to as 'back' motivated. If they have a product that either moves slow or not at all, they can tell you exactly how many times they have hauled that product in and out of their vehicle. Dealers will happily break their backs moving product into the show. As the show draws to a close the motivation changes and the thought of moving that product back out to their van or car starts to weigh heavily upon their back.

To promote your local show, don't rely solely on telling people as they come into your store. The main reason after all if to generate new customers for your store. You need to advertise the show well. Radio spots, newspaper advertisements, swapping advertising with other local businesses are all good ways to spread the word. Contact your local television station and find out if the news department would cover the event. Check with your local professional sports teams and get one or more of the athletes to come to the show to sign autographs. Many athletes are connected to a charity. If you present them with the opportunity to sign autographs to raise money for their charity, often they will come to your show at no charge to you. Just remember to keep in mind that the main purpose of the show is to promote your store. If the show itself breaks even you're money ahead. You will have made your profit from the tables of your own product sold at the show. The primary benefit comes later as you generate new customers and keep your current ones happy and excited about collecting.

As a storefront owner or dealer there are several types of customers you will learn to deal with very quickly. The methods in dealing with them vary, but one thing remains the same no matter the collector. Their way of collecting, what they collect, and who they collect is the best, and the rest is trash.

Casual Fan vs. Avid Fan: The casual fan will never bring a lot of business through your door. If a casual fan of Dan Marino walks into your store, he just wants to own something that is a Dan Marino item. He may buy a one-dollar trading card, or a three-hundred dollar autographed helmet. Once he has bought his one item he is done and won't be back until there is a new team or player to which he wishes to connect through an object.

The avid fan is the complete antithesis of the casual fan. Like a bag of potato chips, 'One is never enough.' To stay with Dan Marino for a moment, the avid fan would have to own every trading card that ever came out with Dan's name or face gracing the front or back. To not own them all would make him sleepless at night. Going to shows, and stores becomes a quest that rivals the search for the Holy Grail. The search especially becomes frantic and desperate as there are fewer and fewer cards he does not own. The fewer cards left to complete his sacred task the lesser the results from his travels. Indeed, once the player retires and there will be no new cards made with his likeness, the light at the end of the tunnel shines brightly. The problem I've seen with these collectors is that once the player has retired, and there are no new cards, they don't know what to do once the set is complete. After spending years tracking down every Dan Marino card ever made, what do you do on that last day after his retirement and you just found and bought the last card? Going from store to store, searching the internet, going to shows, making phone calls, doing trades, becomes a way of life. When the last card is bought the avid fan often gets bored and becomes an avid fan of someone else and starts the cycle all over again. What many of them never figure out is that their excitement is derived from the challenge of finding all the cards, not necessarily in the possessing. Trading cards, as with much else in life, is driven by the thrill of the chase, not the thrill of possession. Many avid fans get around this problem of players retiring by being an avid fan of a team. The team, unless moved to another city, will always be there and will always generate more cards to chase. There are many collectors that will wish to complete sets of all the trading cards of players from the team for each year. The problem these fans have is finding the cheapest cards. Most dealers don't take common cards to shows. Since most common cards are only worth a nickel to a quarter they are not considered worth the effort of hauling them in and out of the show, and not worth the cost of table rent to furnish them a spot on your table. As a storefront owner the best thing you can do for them is put their sets together for them. If you are doing a show and someone makes a request, take the information, fill the request at your store, and arrange the terms and shipping. If you are able to help them find the common cards that they need, you will gain a regular customer.

The Casual Collector vs. The Serious Collector: The casual collector is an easy person to please. As with the casual fan, the casual collector rarely spends more than a few dollars here and there. The casual collector will wish, on occasion, to buy the modestly priced card that makes them go ooh and ah. The casual collector is after cards that are appealing to the eye, and unusual in their dazzling special effects.

The serious collector is quite the opposite. Though they may appreciate the look of the prisms, refractors, and the like, it is the return on investment that drives these collectors. When a person buys cards as a true investment they are looking at a card and making a determination as to whether or not they will be able to realize a profit from that card down the road. There are two standard forms of investing in cards, long term and short term. If a collector is looking for a short term return on their investment they are banking that the value of the card will increase over the course of that players' active career. They will want to sell the card at the peak of the popularity of the player. Rookie cards are excellent for this type of collector. Most players will see their cards decrease in value once they retire. Because of this known trend the cards of most players are like a hot potato. The card will peak as their career peaks and will decline in value as their career declines. The last person holding the card will take the largest hit on depreciation. Long term investing is as much luck as it is skill if you really want to cash in on the largest profits. A collector investing for the long term will want to purchase cards of a future hall of fame inductee that is also a superstar in the here and now. A perfect example is the rookie card of Michael Jordan. In 1986 when Fleer released the wax packs containing his rookie card they sold for about two dollars a pack. At the time his card was just another of the many rookie cards in the set. A person in 1986 would have been able to buy a wax box containing thirty-six packs of 1986-87 Fleer for somewhere in the neighborhood of fifty dollars. That same box would be worth well over five thousand dollars today. One pack out of the box can sell anywhere from one hundred dollars to two hundred dollars. The reason is that the rookie card of Michael Jordan is valued at well over one thousand dollars for a merely average card. A perfect card with a PSA rating of ten can go as high as five thousand dollars. That investment, made in 1986, has realized a return of more than one-hundred percent per year over the twelve years from then to his retirement.

Pests and Know-it-alls: Every industry has them and collecting is no different. They know more than anyone else, collect better things than anyone else, and knows better than anyone what an item is worth. At least that's what they believe. Some are friendly and simply wish to enlighten you on the ways of the business. They want to help you by giving you inside information or insights into what is going to happen with the careers of the players. After all, John Elway always calls this guy before the big game to give him the inside scoop, doesn't he? There are however the other know-it-alls, the ones that are rude and abusive. You will find them more often at shows than you will in your own store. I suppose it's because they don't know you and assume they will never see you again. They will look at a few cards in which they have interest and proceed to help you understand more fully the phrase, 'raked over the coals'. They will rant and rave to you how your cards aren't worth anything and that they know what it's worth and you're trying to gouge them. Their speech can be more than colorful at times and is certainly not something you need to entertain. The theory of never seeing you again goes both ways. This person isn't in your store and most likely doesn't know that you have a store. The level of abuse you feel you need to tolerate can drop dramatically with a person such as this. There is no need for you to stoop to his level, but it is a simple thing to remind the Neanderthal that no one is forcing him to buy anything and if he doesn't like the price he can keep on walking. Do it politely and in a calm tone and you will frustrate his entire day. Drop to his level and bluster right back at him and he will feel vindicated and justified in his behavior.

Of all of them the one that will grate the most on your nerves is the one with his own Beckett price guide. He will smugly pull that guide out of his back pocket and proceed to look up the price for each and every card in which he has interest. The process is exquisite in its inhuman torture. After spending an hour or more with this person you will long for your next Dentist visit. After challenging you on a price you will remind him that his price guide is several months old and it would be to his benefit to purchase a new guide. Undaunted by your irritating use of logic he will proceed to use his price guide to value your cards. Imagine the glee with which you would be greeted by an antique automobile owner when you pull out a used car guide from 1960 that lists his 1957 T-Bird at a few hundred dollars.

Other Dealers: Selling product to other is an opportunity many dealers never realize. The product that moves slowly for you may move wonderfully for them. Prior to the start of a show, grab some of your slow moving cards and shop them around to the other dealers. Keep in mind that they will need to buy it from you at a price that will allow them to make a profit. If you have a card valued at one-hundred dollars and you are in a state which sells consistently at half-book the dealer will only be able to get fifty dollars when he sells the card. That means you will need to sell it to him for twenty-five dollars or less. You get to liquidate a slow mover and he gets to make a profit. Don't make the mistake of holding onto stock forever that doesn't move. As I've said before, the card business is a game of hot potato, so don't be the last one holding the card when the price falls.

The primary thing to keep in your mind when selling collectibles is to keep it fun. If you can keep the hobby of collecting new, exciting, and fun for your customers and for you, it can be one of the most enjoyable businesses to own and operate. This business of collecting will tie you to your customers as no other. The relationship to your customers will be far more of a personal nature than of any other storefront. The opportunities to tie yourself tightly into your community are far greater than with any other business. A city or town may have thousands of businesses but when it comes to their sports teams, they all come together as one community. Sports connects people as few other things in our society can. By tapping into that feeling of connection you have a rare opportunity, don't waste it, and don't take it too seriously. As a friend of mine once said, "It's all cardboard."

CHAPTER ELEVEN

▼

WHOLESALE BUSINESSES

There are aspects of wholesale business that apply to any business dealing with other businesses, so I'll say again…NOOOOOOOOOOOOOOOOOO skipping chapters!!! They all apply to your business, and if you think they don't, just wait until you get to the next chapter, and you'll be sooorrrrrry!

If you wholesale a product to other businesses, you either produced the product or you didn't. If you produce the product you are going to sell wholesale, you need to ask yourself a very important question…"Is it a good idea for me to take on the dual role of producer and wholesaler?" There will be three main things to examine in order to answer this question.

1. If I take on both roles, can I sell enough product to match my production?

2. If I produce only, can my production meet the demands of my wholesaler?

3. If I take on both roles, will my production keep up with my sales?

If your production capability is limited, you may not be able to meet the product demands that a wholesaler may require. In that case, you may be able to effectively produce and sell the product. If your production capacity is limited, you will have four options sitting in front of you:

1. Contract with a wholesaler—this wholesaler will represent your product for you. This will allow you to spend more time producing your product. It may mean expanding your production to meet the demands of the wholesaler, so you may need a source of funds to expand your production capacity.

2. Sell it yourself—you will be splitting your time between production and sales, so it may take some time for either to grow appreciably. Be prepared for a lower rate of growth with this option. The upside is that you will have your hand actively in both, so growing pains should be minimized.

3. Contract the production—you can act as the wholesaler, and not be limited by a small production capacity. The upside is that you won't have the capital expense of gearing up a larger production capability. The downside is that you will need to be very sure that the product is consistently produced to your specifications and satisfaction.

4. Contract production and wholesaling—by contracting both sides, you will essentially take on the role of quality control and promoter. The upside is that you have professionals on both sides of you, and you can gain tremendously from that. It will also allow you the time to hit the trade show circuit and promote your product like a madman. The downside is that both sides are out of your direct day to day control. This means you will need to be ever vigilant to ensure that the quality of the product is maintained, and that your customers are served to their satisfaction. I hope you've caught onto the fact that I never say that customers should be served to 'your' satisfaction. Customers should always be served to THEIR satisfaction. If you

take care of your customers, your customers will take care of you. Old cliché, but very true.

If you don't produce the product(s) you sell, you can still be one of three basic types of wholesaler:

1. As in our discussion above, you may be a gun for hire. This requires a thorough knowledge of the market in which you intend to participate. You will need to know what types of products will be movers in the industry, and know who your clients will be for any given product. You can approach the client base from two possible directions. The first is that you find a great product...who the clients will be....and then go and get the orders. The second is that you have an established clientele, have an intimate knowledge of their needs, and you go out seeking product that will fit your client base. From either approach, the need to be tuned in to the producers is critical. You will need to convince them why you are the one to represent their product to the industry. You will also be fighting the inevitable desire of the producer to bring the wholesale function in-house. The number of times a wholesaler gets a product off the ground...just to have the producer then yank the product back in-house is one incredibly large number. Most of the time the sales of the product drop once it's brought in-house., but the dollar signs become hard for the producer to ignore. The temptation to look at the sales as a zero sum game becomes a trap in which many producers get caught. They look at the sales you generate and the margin that is going to your business. They then get the idea that the money going to your company is money coming out of their pocket. I had experience with one company in which they were paying the company for which I worked in the neighborhood of $80,000 a year in commissions to sell their product. The product was still in the growth curve of it's sales and our company was on track to hit $100,000 in commissions. The producer started thinking about how nice $100,000 more on his

bottom line would look on his books. The day came that the producer decided to pull the product and internalize the sales effort. Why had they pulled the product? Could it have been stopped? Did the move pay off for the producer? The answers are easy and obvious, but require communication and a little 'blowing your own horn' promotion. They pulled the product because the management of the wholesaling company never went back to the producer on a regular basis and said, "Here's what we're doing for you." The wholesaler simply turned in orders. Anyone can do that! But it leaves the producer to think there was nothing involved in getting those orders. You need to make sure the producer knows how hard you're working to promote their product. Show them how many contacts you're making, your success rate per call, the growth of each customer, and how much you're putting on the bottom line of the producer. You need the producer to feel that he will make more money with you getting a piece of the pie that he will with you out of the loop. Could the yanking of the product have been stopped? Not once the decision is made. When your company is finally notified by the producer of their intention to internalize the sales of the product, you're too late. They have already set up the internal structure to handle the product by the time they yank it back. Keeping the sales effort external of the producer will be a constant vigil on your part. Keep the producer happy and overwhelmed at all times. Blow your own horn every chance you get, and make the producer feel that the job is far too big for them to handle. Did the move pay off for the producer? Not even close. The producer sold the same product to another industry, but had no experience in the industry to which the wholesaler had been selling their product. They didn't know the contacts beyond the name on an order form. When their sales force tried to move into this industry, their focus was naturally diluted from their main industry. As their force was diluted, the management decided to become passive in this industry and reassert their focus in their main industry. Passive selling is about as successful as passive sports. How many touchdowns would you score if you were busy working on your basketball game while the other team was playing football? The cost per sale increased for the producer, and their market share declined. Not a good combination for success. So...what can we glean from what happened? Both sides lost in this situation. The producer did not value the service the wholesaler was performing...with respect to the selling of the producer's product. But, was that the fault of the producer? Most certainly not. As a wholesaler, you have to make your value known over and over and over again. Show them that you have value, and that you are putting money into their pocket. As with any business, profit is the bottom line. Don't rely on a personal relationship with the producer to carry the day. The last thing you want to hear from a producer who is also a friend is, "Just business, nothing personal." Even if you develop a friendship with a producer, the profit of the producer will make the final decision as to the continued retention of your company. If the producer believes his bottom line will be larger without you, you will be gone quickly and with no remorse.

2. The second type of wholesaler is also the gun for hire, but is quite different in that he only represents one producer. This is not an uncommon practice, and many wholesalers that start small take this approach. There will be two essential types of businesses that would be candidates for your services. The first would be a company that is small and looking to find representation to break into the market. The second is an established company that has produced for itself, and is either interested in selling their products wholesale, or could be convinced to do so. With either type of company the benefit is that having no current presence in the wholesale market, you can both grow together. The benefit, however, is also the drawback. You will be introducing products to the industry that are new and must

be proven. You will have to create the market for these products. It can be a terribly exciting challenge, but a great responsibility as well. The producer, not knowing what to expect, will look intently on what you are doing, and most likely will be overly anxious about the results. You will need to be extraordinarily attentive to the producer to allay their fears and keep their continued confidence. Work out a reporting schedule with them as to how often they would like updates and progress reports. If they want them every week, you may cringe at the time it takes away from selling, but it is just as important to hold the hand of the producer as it is to get the sale. It is especially important when this producer is your only supplier. The last thing you want is to lose your only source of product. The good news is that if you do everything correctly, this one on one relationship will be a very profitable one. With your success, the producer will be highly motivated to supply you with as much product as you can move. The producer also has the benefit of time saved. He only has to deal with you for the wholesaling of all of his products. Most producers have to deal with a myriad of wholesalers, which can take a bit out of their efficiency.

3. The third type of wholesaler is a storefront wholesaler. Of these, there are two basic types: the 'Open to the Public' wholesaler and the one that sells only to retailers. A quick personal note to those of you thinking of opening the 'Open to the Public' operations. I, and a lot of other people that have been…or are in…retail, simply won't buy from wholesalers who open their doors to the public. It creates a lot of problems for the retailers and we will delve into those problems shortly. If you are opening a wholesale storefront for retailers only, location is very important. You want to be convenient to your retailers, but the last place you want to locate in is a heavy retail traffic area. If you locate your wholesale business geographically close to your retailers, their customers will catch sight of your store eventually, and

will begin to associate you with lower prices and the retailers with high prices. As consumers, we don't often wonder as to the wholesale price of an item while we are shopping. But, if the wholesaler of the item is in clear view, the idea begins to move to the forefront of our thoughts. Therefore, while it is important to be close to your retailers, you don't want to be too close or too visible. If, however, your intention is to open a wholesale storefront that is also open to the public, be prepared for the bulk of your business to be from the public, and not the retailers. When you sell to retailers, they are often buying multiple quantities of any particular item. When products are purchased in a bulk format, as by a retailer, your cost per unit decreases. This allows you to sell at a price considered wholesale. You make your profit by smaller margins, but large volumes. Once you open your doors to the public, that all goes away. The public will typically only be buying one of a particular product, increasing your cost of merchandising to that of a retailer. You will have established a two or three tier pricing system, most likely using some sort of code. With the pricing code, the public won't know how much the retailer pays for the product, so everyone is happy….right? Unlikely. Your initial cost is lower than that of a retailer, so you will fall into the same trap every other 'Open to the Public' wholesaler that I have ever seen tumbles. You need to move product, you have fewer retailers that purchase product from you than a 'retailer only' wholesaler, so you target the public. You can't sell to the public at a true wholesale price, or you would go out of business. Your cost would be too high per piece, and you would lose money on each item sold. You can't sell product to retailers at a retail price because once they mark up the product, they would be stuck with an overpriced inventory. So…into what trap does every 'Open to the Public' wholesaler fall? They move the two basic price structures closer together. Since the cost per item is higher than a true wholesaler (due to selling a piece at a time to the public), they raise the price to wholesalers. They also drop the price to the public to a price below retail. They move the wholesale and retail price closer together in an attempt to keep as many retailers as possible and, at the same time, bring in a large public following. But what is the effect on the retailers that purchase product from you for their stores? Since you charge them more than a true wholesaler does, they must either accept less margin on those products, or mark them up above what the retail market will bear. Neither is a desirable option to your retail customers. The other problem they have is one of familiarity of product. Your retail customer will have to listen to customers come into their store and say, (either to them or to another shopper) "That's the same thing I saw at XYZ Wholesale, and it was only $12.00 there. The stuff here must all be overpriced!" If that happens just one time in your retail customer's store, I guarantee that you will never get them back as a client. The damage done to that retail customer is too great for them to risk bleeding customers away because the customer will assume they are overpriced on all of the product they sell. Consumers don't truly acknowledge a distinction between wholesale and retail. When a customer views product in your quasi-wholesale store, you will have set the price and the worth in the mind of that customer. They will not then walk into the store of one of your retail customers and understand that it is more expensive here because this store is retail and yours is wholesale. If you feel you must have public traffic, be honest about your intentions. Don't play the game of trying to be in both markets. If you desire to be truly wholesale, then be truly wholesale. Find out from your retail customers how much they mark up their product on average. Once you have that information, mark up your product to the public by that same margin. The public will still feel as if they are getting a bargain because they will see the word 'wholesale' on your building. It never fails that a shopper will pay more for a product than they would normally if they see the words 'Outlet', 'Factory Direct', or 'Wholesale' on your building. Supposed 'Outlets' have made a killing off of uneducated shoppers that herd themselves in like sheep just to get a chance to grab hold of an 'Outlet' bargain. At the same time, make the cost of your product to your retail customers truly wholesale. This will allow them the proper markup so that they can make an acceptable profit. It will also change the comments in their store to, "Wow, they sell for the same price as that wholesale place." That comment will keep the retail customer coming back to you for product.

Whichever of these ways you decide to set up your wholesale storefront, make sure to canvass the area for customers. Send mail, faxes, phone calls, postcards, or anything else it takes for the retail stores in the area to find out about you. Advertise your wholesale facility on the Internet in an attempt to solicit business outside your area. Check out your local library and look at copies of books that list wholesalers. Contact the publisher or the agency that lists the wholesalers, and get yourself onto their lists. Go to your library and look at the telephone books from across the country, and begin soliciting businesses that would be interested in your products. The name of the game is exposure. The wider your customer base, the more steady and solid will be your business. Your local library can be a wealth of information. You can also go to the magazine section and look up organizations that would be of benefit to you. Retail associations, wholesale associations, and import/export associations can all be of tremendous benefit. Attend trade shows for these organizations as your schedule allows. Trade shows can be sources of new product for your wholesale operation or avenues to find more customers. Market, market, market, and then market some more. As I said before, go in with the attitude "If the world isn't buying from me, they're stupid!"

Well...you're in the home stretch. ::::::rubbing your shoulders:::::: you can make it champ. All that's left is the mechanics of start-up and a wrap-up. You can do it slugger...just one more round...errrr...chapter, and you got it licked. So...turn the page champ, and let's finish this thing off and go home!

It's ummm…that way champ →   →   →   →

::::::scratches head:::::: must be a little punch drunk. I'll help you a bit…you must be getting tired ::::::holds your two fingers:::::: We grab the page by the corner…that's it…and then we…

CHAPTER TWELVE

MECHANICS

...lift...you did it!

Can you believe it? We are actually in the last chapter. I'm just so proud that you're still here...::::::sniff, sniff::::::

You haven't been scared away yet I see. You know what kind of business you want to open. You know how to market the business. You know the do's and don'ts of customer service. You've got a name for the business all picked and ready to go, and you know how you're going to structure the legal entity that is the company (in case you forgot, that's sole proprietorship, LLC, S corporation, or C corporation).

Were you wondering why you needed to read all of the chapters, even though your business will fit into one of the categories? If you have been wondering, shame...shame...shame on you. I told you in chapter five that I would tell you how to control those nasty seasonal cycles. So brace yourselves...here it comes. In today's exceedingly competitive markets, there is no longer such a thing as a company that can survive by living wholly within one category. So you get a gold star if you stood up and shouted,

"We have to do them all!" The category of your company will be the primary category, not the only category. If you are a retail store, you need to be on the Internet, have the customer service of a service company, the attention to detail of a wholesaler, the fun environment of a flea marketer, and the home service of a mail order company. If you intend to compete successfully, you must integrate all of these into your business, and take from each of them the properties that will enhance the business you have chosen. If you intend to make the cycles work for you and stabilize your cash flow, then you need to incorporate all six of these businesses into you own. Mail order and Internet stores can even out the cash flow of your storefront. For those of you who will operate stores that can't sell through mail order or the Internet, they can still be excellent lead generators. Bringing all of them together into your store will allow you to even out your cash flow by bringing new business to you all year long, as opposed to the times of the year when your business would normally peak.

So…let's start this puppy up and get it hummin'!!! What in the world do you do to get the company operational after you know everything else? We're going to cover this in list form so, if you need to, just copy this list, or check them off in the book as you get them done. Some of the things will not apply to all businesses, so if something doesn't apply to your business, just skip over it and move on to the next item.

1. Find a printer that does exceptional artwork and design. Yes, believe it or not, I have the printer and designer listed first. You won't know what to clear at the trademark office until you actually have a logo on which to run a search. And, unless you have extraordinary talent, you will need someone to design your logo(s) and the 'look' for your company name. It will be in your interest to have a few designs you like as backups for your first choice. By having a backup, you don't have to worry about a time consuming re-design, should your first choice for logo not clear the trademark office.

2. Clear the name(s) and logo(s) you intend to use. Check with federal and state officials to ensure that your company name(s) and logo(s) are clear for use. Once it is determined that they are clear for use you will need to copyright, trademark, and register them immediately. For federal registration contact the trademark and patent office. For state registration contact the office of the State's Attorney General. Often your local library will have an office that can perform these searches for you, but you will still need to fill out the paperwork yourself to get your company protected.

3. Find a business attorney. Even if you only send him a Christmas card once a year, you need to have an attorney. Make sure his specialty is business or corporate law. You want him to be able to assist you in all your business matters, not just the creation of the legal shell of the business.

4. Set up the legal entity of the business. Whether it be a sole proprietorship, a limited liability company, a S corporation, or a C corporation, make sure to get this done before you go any further.

5. Get an accountant that accepts start-up businesses. Don't even attempt to try and figure out what tax forms you will need to file now that you are a business. It will be inexpensive compared to the significant hours you would be taking away from your work to do the same task.

6. Open a business checking account. You will need to have authorized the bank you have chosen to act as your depositor, so make sure to have that done when you establish your legal shell. Select checks that will serve the dual role of paying bills and paying payroll. This way you won't have to purchase a set of checks for each type of transaction.

7. Establish your phone, fax, and toll free numbers. You will need these before you can sell the first thing or print the first business card.

8. Establish your e-mail address and web site address. Get these addresses committed, even if you won't be writing the website for some time. By getting a domain name now, you will be able to include it in your literature, and on your business card. Don't worry that the site isn't actually doing anything yet. It is a simple thing to put a logo on the site and a phrase asking them to come back, or that the site is under construction. And remember to use a free e-mail host such as Hotmail or Yahoo. By doing this your e-mail address will stay the same regardless of the Internet service provider that you decide to use.

9. Literature. Design all of the literature that you intend to use in your business. Flyers, brochures, business cards, coupons, mailers, post-cards, thank you cards, sales forms, invoices, statements, reporting forms, letterhead, promotional sheets, expense forms. Sit down and really think through every possible form or type of material that you will need and get it all done ahead of time. This will allow you to hit the road running, rather than always having to get this printed or that designed.

10. Purchase the equipment you will need. If you are in retail, you may be able to find some of your office equipment wholesale. One of the advantages of having a retail merchant license is that no one need know that you don't sell fax machines in your store to buy just one from a wholesaler. Decide what equipment you need, and get it done now.

11. Establish your suppliers. If you need product, find out from where you will get that product. Try and establish terms that are beneficial to you if possible. Once you have found them, never stop looking for new suppliers.

12. Displays. If you will have a booth at a trade show, or have need of a display in your store, design them now. They can be made very quickly or take months, according to the artwork and the design time going into the display. This will represent your company to the people, so unless you have no choice do not go cheap on your displays. They make an incredible impression when they are done exceptionally well.

13. Cash Register. This will be an important tool for your business. Secure one that will perform all of the functions you need done on a daily basis. Cash registers today range from simplistic to sophisticated. If you need dual receipts, don't purchase one that only produces one receipt. If you want daily reports, make sure it has that feature. The point I'm trying to make is that there are so many cash registers on the market today, don't settle for one that has 'most' of the features you feel you will need. Go to a business that sells cash registers rather than going to an office supply store. By going to a business that sells nothing but cash registers, you will have a much wider selection, and be much happier with your purchase.

14. Accepting credit cards. These days, I would be hard pressed to think of a business that shouldn't accept credit cards. Unless you're doing deals in the millions of dollars, where letters of credit are used to ensure payment, you will need to accept credit cards. There are a lot of companies that offer credit card service and equipment. Do your homework before deciding which to use. Do the math when comparing monthly fees, per transaction fees, percentage of purchase fees, purchase versus leasing fees for the equipment, phone-in fees, key entry fees, debit fees, and any other fee they can think of to charge to you. Find the one that will give you the best price for the best service. If you will be using a cash register, you may want to consider purchasing a cash register that has the credit card swipe mechanism in the register itself. It saves on counter space, as opposed to having the separate credit card box on the counter as well as the cash register.

15.Check verification. Sooner or later someone is going to bounce a check. The benefit of knowing that before the customer takes possession of the product is that you don't get stung. Even if you don't operate a storefront, check verification is never a bad idea. I've known businesses to ship a load of product, get a check for ten or twenty thousand dollars, and spent the next few years trying to collect the money after the check bounced. As always, compare companies to get the best rate and the best service.

16.Buy a safe. Whatever size of safe you need, make sure it's fireproof. Being fireproof is relative, so check the ratings on the safe. Most of you will buy a small floor safe, and these are rated by how long they will protect the documents they contain from burning. Get the longest fire protection for the size you need. If you protect nothing else, protect the documents that describe the legal shell of your company. If you filed as a corporation, protect your share certificates, you incorporation papers, and all the minutes from all your corporate meetings. If you need to be able to store cash or have a one way safe, make it separate from your documents safe. A one way safe is one in which cash can be deposited by one of your employees, but they can't access it to remove any cash. Whatever you do, deposit cash daily. Don't make your safe a rich and tempting target. Employees will know how often you empty the safe. If you regularly take too long between deposits, you may get plucked by one of your employees somewhere down the road.

17.Location. Choose the location for your business based upon the criteria we reviewed earlier in the book.

18.Signs. What signs will you place on the building? Will there be a sign along the road? Will there be signs for the interior of your business? Find a reputable sign maker in your area that will come out to your store and assist you in the design. Their input will be crucial in helping you to design signs that will accomplish what you want for a price you can afford.

19. Surveillance and security. Even if you operate out of your home, you should have a security system. Your customer contacts and histories are too important to risk by not having a security system. In regards to home security, one of the most important pieces of the system will be the sign in your front yard. It's low tech, but very effective. Most burglars are not very good, and will choose to move on to a home without a security system, rather than run the risk of testing their skills. If you operate your business out of your home, you REALLY need a security system. Your business will more than likely be vacant more than it is occupied, so protecting it and your information is vital. Surveillance can be very important, not only in catching the criminal, but in deterrence. If the criminal thinks you're going to see his face, he will often think twice about doing something illegal. This works for employees as well. Maintaining a surveillance camera on a vital area of your business can be beneficial if you have 'snooping' employees who like to see documents that they have no business seeing, or enter offices that they have no business entering. If you operate a wholesale or retail storefront, security is important, but surveillance is a must. I don't care how good a job you do hiring your employees, at some point one or more of them is going to succumb to temptation and skim money. Your surveillance should not only be directed at the store floor to catch shoplifters, but at the cash registers as well, to make sure your employees remain honest. Let your employees know they are there, and give them the benefit of, hopefully, resisting all temptation. There are always the few who know they are being watched, but think they will be able to be sneaky enough to not be caught by the camera. Most however, will not even make the attempt once they are aware of the camera.

20. Liability insurance. Unless you operate from your home, and no one will ever come to your home on a business matter, you will need liability insurance. Don't even think that your homeowner's insurance

will cover a claim if they find out it was business related. If you get only occasional traffic, a standard million-dollar policy will be adequate. If your business will receive heavy traffic, there is no such thing as a policy that is too big in our lawsuit happy country. Make sure your policy covers anything for which your company could be considered liable. Injuries, harassment, discrimination, not turning your head when you sneeze, or maybe you didn't provide the proper donut assortment last Wednesday. There are a myriad of reasons for which a company could be sued, so make sure your policy covers them all.

21. Contents insurance. The policy needs to be sufficient in size, not only for your current contents, but also for your growth. Otherwise, you will be constantly calling to increase your coverage. This policy will need to cover all of your equipment, office supplies, inventory, and everything down to the coffee grounds. Keep a detailed list of everything your company owns, including inventory, in your safe. Once you make the list, don't just tuck it away and forget about it. Update it every time you purchase a substantial item. Update the list regularly with regard to inventory as well.

22. Trade associations. These will have enormous value to you. Get yourself into as many free ones as you can find, and as many that cost money as you can afford. The contacts you can make when you become an active participant are phenomenal and can pay huge dividends.

23. Attitude of your store. Your store will take on a personality. Will that personality be reserved? Will it be light-hearted? Will it be a circus type atmosphere? This will need to be something you think about long and hard, and set into motion. The atmosphere of the store will eventually begin to attract the type of customer who has an affinity to that atmosphere.

24. Inventory. Get the product ordered and sitting in the store. Straightforward and simple.

25. Advertising. Design it all. Newspaper, radio, television, Internet, banner exchanges, mutual, and cooperative. Get them all designed, recruited, and in place for the day you open. Are you going to hold events? Will they be in the store? Will there be out of the store events? Get them planned before opening day.

26. Design your customer service and incentives programs. Have them ready to roll the day you talk to your first customer.

27. Bonding. If the business you will open requires you be bonded, get it done before you open. If you are going to hire employees that will be performing services that require bonding, make sure you get them bonded before they see their first customer.

28. Unemployment insurance. You will need to contact your state's unemployment office to register your company, so that you will be in compliance with the payroll laws of your state. If you have even one employee, you will be required to pay unemployment insurance based upon your company's payroll. Unfortunately most, if not all, states will even require you to pay unemployment on any salary you draw from the company.

29. Property insurance. You will only need this if you own the building and the property. If you do, get it covered for everything allowed. Don't pass on flood insurance just because (no matter how much it rained) you don't think the water would get to you. Flood insurance generally covers water damage caused by burst pipes as well.

30. Workman's compensation insurance. This will only cover your employees, not you. Law requires it, and you'll be hit hard if you don't obtain the insurance, and an employee gets hurt on the job. Don't take it lightly, thinking that your employees don't perform

dangerous tasks, so you would never have need of it. If an employee slipped on the floor and broke his or her neck, you would probably be out of business by the time everyone was done suing you. Get the insurance so that your business is protected. The insurance company providing your liability and contents insurance will also be able to provide this insurance as well.

31. Rider to cover. As the owner, you will need a rider to cover you under workman's comp insurance. Make sure and get it, because if you are hurt at work, your personal health insurance won't cover your medical bills.

32. Wearable and promotional goods. If your business will require a uniform, shirts, jackets, hats, or promotional items, make sure to get them ordered and in your possession before you open your doors. You should also decide if your business would be such that customers would purchase your wearable and promotional goods. Some companies use wearable and promotional items as gifts for customers as well. Whether or not you decide to sell them, give them away, or supply them only to employees, get it done before you open your doors.

33. Employee posters. Federal law requires that if you have even one employee, you must place posters describing the laws regarding minimum wage and equal opportunity. Your state may also have poster requirements. Check with your state and federal business offices to obtain these posters. They must be displayed in an area of your business in which your employees can see them on a regular basis.

34. Payroll service. I highly recommend hiring a service to handle your entire payroll. They will write the checks, calculate the taxes to be pulled from the checks, and calculate your state and federal deposits. Some will even make the deposits for you, but I personally have always had a hard time giving someone else access to my business accounts.

::::::Whew:::::: I need to cool down for a minute. I think we've got it all covered, but as with any business, there are always things that pop up from time to time that you never would have anticipated. Don't rush in an attempt to get your doors opened quickly. You will be far better off in the long run to have taken the extra time preparing for your first day of business. Laying the proper foundation for your company will allow you to focus on the task at hand, which is selling. If you open for business with things left undone, you will be in a constant start and stop mode, always having to stop selling to take care of something that should have been done before you opened for business. My grandfather was a carpenter, and he always stood by something he told me that every carpenter must be required to memorize while learning his trade, "measure twice, cut once." It's a saying we have all most likely heard, but pay little heed to in today's hurried world. It's a saying that, in those four short words, says all that needs to be said about preparation. It says that it's better to take the extra time to ensure that the job is done right the first time. Taking extra time to do it right before you open will save you time down the road. I promise you that any pre-opening, preparatory work will take much longer after you have opened for business than it would have before you opened for business.

Whether it's before you open for business or after, if you have done your homework, and you know your business, trust your instincts. Believe in yourself. Lower your head, charge into the fray, and be too bull-headed to know any better. Another of my grandfather's quotes that has stuck with me to this day was, "If it doesn't fit, get a bigger hammer." It sounds very comical, but sometimes it's not a bad idea. If your company doesn't 'fit' in the marketplace because of tough competition, a glutted market, or low demand, get a bigger hammer, and just keep pounding until you fit and someone else no longer fits. Find the angle, the hook, the program, or whatever else you wish to call it, and keep hitting your customers and your competition over the head with it until somebody yells, 'Uncle', and starts buying.

This isn't going to be easy, and if anyone tells you it is, run from them as fast as you can. Go in with the right attitude. Be determined, stubborn, and don't pay attention to anyone that tells you it can't be done. When they tell you to, "Give up, it can't be done," they're lying. It has been done before. People have started businesses. If they didn't, there would be no employees. People started IBM, Ford, General Motors, Microsoft, and Chrysler. These companies didn't start themselves. You'll find nowhere in the bible that says, 'On the sixth day God created AT&T'. Individuals started all of these companies. The individual is what makes this country the greatest in the world. The most powerful force in the world is one individual standing up and shouting to the world, "I have an idea!" When we look back at out history, we don't celebrate groups or countries. We celebrate individual achievement, and rightly so. People that dare greatly, and achieve greatly, inspire us to action. Do we remember the colonial man in our history that sat at home grumbling about those darned British? It is more likely that we remember a young man standing before a crowd shouting, "Give me liberty or give me death!" We learn the words because of the individual who spoke the words.

"It can't be done!" When you hear these words, they are saying that you can't get it done. It is up to you to decide whether or not they are right. Some people are not cut out for the challenge of owning and operating their own business. But, if you are up to the challenge, there will be no greater reward, no greater satisfaction, than looking back on what you have created. Take the words from all the people that tell you that you can't do it, and cherish their words. Use them as your inspiration. Allow their words to spur you on to success. Stand up and tell the world, "I can and I will do this!" Bring your company into being through your sheer force of will. Building your company will be unlike anything you have ever built before. The actual business is an intangible. A business has assets, but they are not the business. Ford has manufacturing plants, but they are not the business. A company may have billions of dollars in assets, but if someone doesn't buy the product, all they have are items for an auction block. The business is the sale, and that is new every day. Your company can be successful today, but if it doesn't have a sale tomorrow, all of the assets in the world mean nothing. Renew your pledge to your customers every day, for they are your business. You will not be in business to sell products or services. You will be in business to make customers happy. If you and your product, or your service make them happy, you have a business!

We've covered a lot of ground in this book, going from just a desire to own a business, all the way to opening the doors. It's up to you to make it succeed. No one else will make it happen for you, and everyone will be waiting with a big, "I told you so," if you fail. Resolve yourself not to fail. You can do this. Have confidence in yourself. And on the days when you feel it all closing in around you, picture the goal and just take one more step. Take upon yourself the attitude that many professional athletes have shown. How many times has an athlete, in obvious pain, simply willed himself to take one more step, shoot one more basket, run one more foot, or make one more play?

So, I will tell you now there will be times when you want to give up. There will be times you will feel you can't go on any longer. But stay focused, keep your eye on the goal, and take one more step, shoot one more basket, run one more foot, and make one more play. You **CAN** do it...you **CAN** make it...and...**YOU WILL BE A SUCCESS!!!**

www.ingramcontent.com/pod-product-compliance
Lightning Source LLC
Chambersburg PA
CBHW030749180526
45163CB00003B/959